THE WAYS OF GOD

THE
WAYS OF GOD

Paths into the New Testament

Harry C. Griffith

MOREHOUSE-BARLOW
Wilton, Connecticut

The author gratefully acknowledges the help of the
Bible Reading Fellowship, 2 Elizabeth St., London
SW1W 9QR, especially for the use of commentary
on Bible passages in Section IV of this book.

Brief quotations from the Bible contained in the text
are ordinarily taken for the *New English Bible,*
copyright © 1961, 1970 by the Delegates of the
Oxford University Press and the Syndics of the
Cambridge University Press.

Morehouse-Barlow Co., Inc.
78 Danbury Road
Wilton, Connecticut 06897

Library of Congress Cataloging-in-Publication Data

Griffith, Harry C.
The ways of God.

1. Bible. N.T. Gospels—Criticism, interpretation,
etc. 2. Jesus Christ—Parables. 3. Bible. N.T.
Galatians—Criticism, interpretation, etc. 4. Jesus
Christ—Person and offices. 5. Christian life—
1960-   . I. Title.
BS2555.2.G69   1986   225.6   85-28785
ISBN 0-8192-1377-2

Printed in the United States of America

2   4   6   8   10   9   7   5   3   1

Contents

SECTION III / Setting Christ Free

SECTION IV / The Heart of the Gospel

Foreword

In J.R.R. Tolkien's *The Fellowship of the Ring,* after the wise Gandalf has explained to the reluctant hero, Frodo, the danger of the age in which they live, Frodo quite honestly says, "I wish it need not have happened in my time."

"So do I," says Gandalf, "and so do all who live to see such times. But that is not for them to decide. All we have to decide is what to do with the time that is given us."

So it is with us. From a spiritual point of view we live in an exciting and yet a perilous time. God seems to be moving in his church, and many congregations are experiencing growth in numbers and in quality of life. There seems little doubt that a spiritual reawakening is sweeping the world.

The bad news is that there continues to be rampant crime, deterioration of the family, drug addiction, racial and social injustice, hunger, violence, pornography—an unending list that evidences a world still desperately in need of a relationship with God.

We Christians have failed, it seems to me, to accomplish our twofold task: that of leading people into life-changing experiences or encounters with God and affirming the normality of a personal relationship with God through Jesus Christ; and that of teaching and training people how to live within that relationship so that they grow daily in the knowledge and love of God, and reflect in their lives the guidance of his Holy Spirit.

The early part of my Christian ministry involved seeing, and helping others to see, "the acts of God"—that vast area of experience which has to do with the individual's personal encounter with Christ. We are in a period of spiritual renewal in which many people have discovered the presence of God in very personal ways. For that we can be grateful; but from our gratitude should flow the acceptance of responsibility.

For each Christian—but especially for those in leadership positions within the church—it is important to understand and to respond positively to "the acts of God" in the lives of others. When Christ breaks through and touches a soul in his special way, that "touch" needs to be reaffirmed. New Christians, or newly awakened ones, may well doubt the reality or the validity of any encounter with God unless they have the reassurance of others.

The more experienced Christian rejoices in what is happening in the life of a friend who has recently encountered the Lord. He listens with keen interest to the new insights his friend has received and the new directions the friend's life is taking. Then, gently and over a period of time, he helps his friend move from the excitement and enthusiasm of experiencing "the acts of God" into an increasingly deeper understanding of "the ways of God".

The purpose of this book is, through Bible study, to assist Christians—"new and old"—in comprehending some of the infinite ways in which God works in the world generally, and specifically in the lives of people.

Four separate types of Bible study are provided, and the material may be used by an individual studying alone, or by a group. It has been my experience, in working with Bible study group leaders around the church, that most groups like a variety of methods of study rather than being trapped in a particular mode of study for too long. Virtually a year of weekly Bible study is provided in this volume.

The book begins with a study of each of five parables of Jesus. The Epistle to the Galatians is then considered, in six sessions, as though it were a letter written by St. Paul to Christians today. There follows an eight-chapter study of characteristics of Christ that are to be manifested in our lives as we are called to "set free" the Christ within us. We conclude with a ten-session look at "the heart of the Gospel"—those passages of Scripture which, in combination, give us a picture of Jesus' life, death, and resurrection. A separate introduction has been prepared for each method of study.

The hope is that individuals and groups using this book will become more conversant with "the ways of God" as we discover the many means by which God would like to be active in our lives. The discussion questions at the end of each chapter focus upon the individual's relationship with God. Thus, the Bible passages are to be seen from a viewpoint of what God is saying to us, through them, that our lives might be changed more perfectly to accord with his purposes for us.

We may be excited or fearful that we live in such times as these, but that is not of great significance. What is important is to decide what to do with the time that is given us.

If we have entered into that liberating experience in which Jesus Christ has become the center of our lives, we have much potential for good because we are capable of fulfilling God's will for us. We can become the very people God calls us to be, serving as his instruments and working out his purposes in a redeemable world.

God expects that of those who call themselves his. We have but to grow in our understanding of, and obedience to, his ways.

H.C.G.

Section I

Parables for Today

Introduction

A story told in a certain way can often reveal truth in greater depth and have more impact upon a person's memory than a direct teaching or a factual account. That, I believe, is why Jesus often taught in parables.

The parables of Jesus are timeless. They speak to us today, revealing truth and making an indelible impression.

For this study, I have chosen several familiar parables. With each, there is an introductory section reflecting a personal experience that ties into the parable. Following the reading of the parable, there is commentary on it, with at least five important points that are supported by Scripture, with each Scripture reference shown.

The person using this study will need to check out each Scripture reference, do a summary of it, and then answer a question applicable to it. There is also a question for reflection at the end of each chapter and a poem (adapted from the writings of the English monk, Father Andrew) illustrating a key teaching in the parable.

Whether this study is undertaken by members of a Bible study group, or by an individual studying alone, each chapter should be approached using the method of study set forth above. By filling in the blanks at the end of each chapter, the book becomes our workbook.

When using this material for group study, the leader simply asks a member of the group what the first scriptural reference said and how he or she answered the question applicable to it. Others are given a chance to add their thoughts, and then another member is asked to respond to the second scriptural reference and question, and so on. Special attention can be given to the question for reflection, if there is time.

The leader should attempt to draw some conclusions, and sum up, at the end of the session; and should make the assignment for the next session.

1

Hidden Treasure

Most people, at one time or another, dream of winning vast prizes or of discovering buried treasure. There is something in us all that likes to get something for nothing.

When I lived in Mississippi, my favorite hobby was collecting rocks. I scoured the creek beds of Yazoo County and found great quantitites of petrified wood, geodes, fossils such as prehistoric sharks' teeth, or simply unusual rocks. I carried backbreaking loads for miles to take my treasures home.

Now that I live in Florida, I am almost as bad about shell collecting. I can't go to the beach without searching the shore for perfect shells of all shapes and colors. I take them home by the bagfull, and my wife, Emily, wonders what to do with them.

Below the surface of my mind, through all my searching, probably lies the hope, never quite expressed, that I will someday find a treasure of immense value, something that will make me vastly wealthy, famous, or both.

Read Matthew 13:44-46. The men in these parables discovered something far more valuable than anything I could find in a creek bed or on a seashore. They found the Kingdom of Heaven.

The Kingdom of Heaven is the world we live in when we truly give our lives to Jesus Christ. There may be turmoil, suffering, and death in our lives, but if we live in the Kingdom of Heaven those things have only a peripheral effect upon us. There is no greater joy than life in the Kingdom of Heaven; it is Heaven on earth. (Luke 12:32-34)

We, as Christians, have seen that we have a choice. We can live in the world and be bound by its temporary nature. Seeing life on earth as all there is, we can do all things for our own satisfaction and be bound by the sins of our chosen condition. (Matthew 19:16-22)

On the other hand, if we choose the Kingdom of Heaven we live in eternity. We see life on earth as a training ground for everlasting communion with God. Everything that was upside down and senseless becomes rightside up and meaningful. Day by day we grow in understanding God's will. (Philippians 3:5-10)

In the parable of the hidden treasure, the man's willingness to sell everything is a picture of total change in a person's life. (Matthew 16:24-26) Once a person has a vision of the Kingdom, he is willing to sacrifice all he has to live in that Kingdom. It is interesting to note that the man sold his possessions joyfully, with no indication that he begrudged his loss or was afraid to lose the things of his past. (Luke 5:27-28)

There is one difference between the parable of the field and the parable of the pearl. In the first, the man happens upon the treasure; in the second, the man seeks it. The first shows us, perhaps, that a man literally can stumble upon the Kingdom even when he is not seeking it. The other parable shows us a man who sought the Kingdom in many places before he found the real thing.

In the parables there is another lesson for Christians. From time to time we will have opportunities to share the treasures of the Kingdom with others—some who are searching and others who are stumbling.

Value is the theme of the parables of the hidden treasure and of the pearl. Specifically, it is the value of the Kingdom of Heaven. Jesus wanted to show us that there is nothing equal in value to life in the Kingdom where we are at one with our Creator and where he does his mighty work through frail people such as you and me.

Check the passages of Scripture referred to above. Summarize each briefly, and then answer the applicable question.

Luke 12:32-34

Summary:

Give a practical example in your own life of "where your treasure is, your heart is also."

Philippians 3:5-10

Summary:

What changes have occurred in your life because of knowing Christ?

Matthew 16:24-26

Summary:

What does Jesus mean by "take up your cross"?

Luke 5:27-28

Summary:

How do you think Levi felt; what was going through his mind and his emotions?

Matthew 19:16-22

Summary:

Why did the man's wealth keep him from the Kingdom of Heaven?

For reflection: Tell of your experience of finding the treasure of the Kingdom of Heaven.

SEEKING GOD

We are, first of all, spiritual people;
Unless we are seeking God first of all,
The basic principle of our lives is wrong.
We were created to glorify God,
And if we do not glorify him—
However pleasant and good-natured our lives may be,
And however many things we may produce in them—
Our lives are failing their true end;
For we were made by God to glorify him
And to enjoy his presence for eternity.

2

Double Standards

I have a friend who was one of the most distinguished judges in the Federal Court system during his tenure of service. He exercised great discretion on the bench, taking every case and all of its ramifications seriously. He never "shot from the hip"; he truly displayed judicial temperament in every case that came before him.

Because I admire him so much, this judge's personal opinions about matters have left an indelible impression upon me. I especially remember how he felt about tax evaders. To him, a person who cheated on his income taxes was one of the most despicable criminals.

For one thing, the risk element is very low in tax evasion compared to other crimes. A person who robs a bank, for instance, is fairly openly committing himself; but the tax dodger had multitudes of ways to cover up his crime, and he knows that it is very unlikely that the amount he has stolen through his cheating would ever be discovered in the first place.

Also, the real tax evader is usually relatively well off financially, and his crime is an act of sheer greed rather than the desperate act of someone uneducated or underprivileged. Finally, the tax criminal steals from us all; the taxes he evades becomes taxes you and I must pay. Viewed from these considerations, it is no wonder that my friend, the judge, felt so strongly about this particular crime.

In my years of law practice I noted another interesting thing about tax evaders: how indignant they are about being caught!

Read Matthew 18:21-35. On the surface, this parable is about forgiveness, or the lack thereof. We tend to want to put "reasonable" limits on the demands that are put upon us, even when the demands come from God. Peter wanted some "reasonable bounds" within which to exercise forgiveness. That, however, is not God's way. (Ephesians 4:32)

Christ intentionally set the debt of the unmerciful servant in the parable at an astronomical figure. He wanted to make it clear that the big debtor in the story had no hope of repaying. His plea for time was ridiculous. We can never repay God for our sins. All we have is already his; what we owe him is our total love and service. (Micah 6:8)

The unmerciful servant had a double standard. It seemed fitting to him that he, a man of importance, should have had allowances made for his mistakes while the little man should bear the full force of the law. It is often thought that the criminal who comes from a "good home" or is affluent should be given a lighter sentence. We tend to have one standard for ourselves, another for everyone else. (Matthew 23:25)

Instead of being grateful for having his debt forgiven, the unmerciful servant reacts with injured pride. He is indignant at having been caught. The key to the parable is in the wrong attitude evidenced by the big debtor. (II Samuel 12:1-9)

Instead of inviting the little debtor to celebrate his good fortune, the unmerciful servant asserts his authority by attacking him. He sees his master's forgiveness as a humiliation instead of an honor. He had placed his confidence in himself and he could not tolerate the collapse of that illusion. We cannot forgive another from the heart until we have come to grips with our own shortcomings. Unless we have a repentant attitude, God's grace can be eternal torment rather than final bliss.

Once again Christ is trying to show us what it is like to live in the Kingdom of Heaven. It is a place where we not only experience forgiveness and grant forgiveness to others, it is where we rejoice at the opportunity to set others free.

The story ends on a somber note. Life is not all "fun and games." We are, after all, accountable for our actions. (Amos 5:11)

The theme of the parable is *ungratefulness*. Our focus is not to be upon how many times we must forgive another, but upon the gratitude we should have for God's continuing and total forgiveness of ourselves.

Check the passages of Scripture referred to above. Summarize each briefly, and then answer the applicable question.

Ephesians 4:32

Summary:

Think of the last time you forgave someone; how did it feel?

Micah 6:8

Summary:

What do these words of Scripture truly mean to you as a Christian?

Matthew 23:25

Summary:

In what area of your life do you have an inconsistency between your "inner" and "outer" attitudes?

II Samuel 12:1-9

Summary:

Has there been an instance in which you had to confront someone "higher" than you? What happened?

Amos 5:11

Summary:

What can you do to help someone less fortunate than yourself during the coming week?

For reflection: Looked at from God's point of view, there is always something the individual is ungrateful about. What area of ingratitude needs to be cleared up in your own life?

Tough Love

The standards of God are irritating to the sinner.
He would like to be left alone with his vices.
He would like to be contented with his own worthlessness.
He would be glad to be spared the "intolerable compliment"
Which God has paid in loving us;
And when some crisis or catastrophe occurs,
He would like it patched up in the most practical way,
With the least possible pain to the person concerned.
But that is not God's way.
God's way is to deal with sin itself.
He would not spare the suffering of his own Son

Because to do so would have thwarted
The eternal purpose of his love.
He may not spare the pain of one of his human children
For the same reason.

3

Growing Up

The first three houses in which Emily and I lived were new, and at each one we had the considerable chore of "starting the yard." When we moved to Florida, we were blessed with a home with a beautiful yard. The former owners had given tender, loving care to their home and to the neatly landscaped grounds.

I soon realized that my busy travel schedule would not leave me time to give my property the care necessary to maintain its former beauty. As time passed, I found that I was fighting a holding action. When the creeping crab grass came along, I knew that I was fighting a losing battle.

Creeping crab grass is an insidious growth. It is rich, bluegreen in color and lies close to the ground and, at first, it is almost pretty. But it spreads rapidly and overtakes the St. Augustine grass. When it has choked or shouldered out everything good, it succumbs to the slightest cold air and lies limp and brown through the winter months.

It only looks dead. In the spring, it comes back with a vengeance, its little roots hanging on to everything with a deadly grip, especially to the roots of the St. Augustine grass. It seems to be immune to weed killers and has to be dug out clump by clump. In desperation I have pulled up more precious St. Augustine grass than crab grass.

Read Matthew 13:24-30, 36-43. The first point in this parable is that Satan is in the business of sowing bad seeds. Unless we guard against him diligently, he sneaks in and spoils the good work we set out to do.

The second point is made by the reaction of the farmer's men. They are typical of those who manifest their faith in a narrow, restrictive way and rush in to destroy the bad regardless of the consequences. (Romans 14:13)

God, however, is patient. He knows that we cannot always distinguish the good man from the bad. Wheat and darnel, in the early stages of their growth, appear to be the same. It takes time for the true nature of a plant or a person to reveal itself. And as plant roots are intertwined, so our lives are interwoven with such a mixture of good and evil that premature separation is not practical. God watches patiently. It is said that he has a back door into the heart of each of us, and there is always the possibility that our good seeds will grow. (Hosea 10:12)

Evil carries with it the seeds of its own destruction, but good is its own reward. In the end, evil will be dealt with, and good will be rewarded. (Galatians 6:7-10)

Only God can judge. (Matthew 7:1-2) There is a crucial difference between the farmer's field and God's field. A wheat seed can produce only wheat, and a darnel seed can produce only darnel. But a bad heart can be transformed into saintliness, and a disciple can turn his back on God. God alone can discern the good and the bad; it is he alone who sees the depth of a human heart and the story of an entire life. (1 Corinthians 4:5)

Judgment is the theme of this parable, specifically the necessity to leave all judgment to God. Our limited perspective and our impatience disqualify us as judges. God alone has the love and the wisdom to judge his children.

Check the passages of Scripture referred to above. Summarize each briefly, and then answer the applicable question.

Romans 14:13

Summary:

What kind of people do you tend to judge most harshly?

Hosea 10:12

Summary:

When would you like God to judge you?

Galatians 6:7-10

Summary:

Do you believe that "good guys never win"?

Matthew 7:1-2

Summary:

Why does judging others cause you to be judged?

I Corinthians 4:5

Summary:

Why should you rejoice that God is your judge?

For reflection: Although we are not to judge one another we all try to make judicious decisions. Think of the person who you would say was the best judge you have known. What were his or her outstanding traits? What does that tell you about yourself?

Choosing

The thoughts we allow to come into our minds and our lives
Are what make our lives what they are.
Just as we can walk on the shady side of the street
Or choose to read trash and see trash and think trash,
So we can walk in the sunshine
And choose to read, see and think what is beautiful.
We have got our free will
And we can, as it were,
Unlock the door to what we will.
We can read what we will, think what we will,
Become what we will.
We are created that we may
Create ourselves.
In the end, if we are faithful, there will emerge
Something like God,
Made not only by God
But by ourselves.

4

Hearing and Doing

I live in a house that is built on sand.

That doesn't concern me, because I know that the engineering skills with which the house was built provide the protection I need. The house can withstand high winds and floods and other natural disasters.

That is my rational side speaking. In my heart I have a problem with sand. I like the hard, rich dirt of my childhood home. To me, there is something impermanent about sand.

My neighbor in Florida moved down from Ohio where his soil was tested regularly for nutritional elements by a soil-testing laboratory. Not knowing of a soil-testing service in Florida, my neighbor sent a sample of his soil to the Ohio laboratory. He asked them to tell him what the Florida soil contained and what fertilizer to use on it. The laboratory replied, "As far as we can tell, you sent us just a bag of sand."

Read Matthew 7:24-27. In the passage, Jesus asks his followers to do two things: to listen and to act. Neither is easy to do, but as the parable demonstrates, failure to heed the warning will result ultimately in disaster. (Proverbs 10:25)

Listening is more than the absorption of sound. When we listen to the words of Jesus, we must be present where his words are spoken; we must be part of his body, the church, and be aware of its teachings, especially those which come from the Bible. (John 15:1-4)

Jesus speaks on a spiritual level, therefore we must listen prayerfully. We should listen expectantly; he did not waste words, and they are vital to our life in him. We should listen sensitively: not only with our ears, but with our eyes (for in his parables Jesus paints pictures for us); not only with our minds but with our hearts. (John 8:31-32)

We cannot be effective disciples unless we listen. We can engage in all kinds of activity, but unless we are doing those things which Jesus would have us do, our time is spent wastefully and perhaps destructively. It is not easy to listen, but Jesus expects it of us. (I Corinthians 3:11)

Jesus calls us also to action. There is little good in learning about Jesus and his teaching if we do not do anything with our knowledge. What we learn has value only when it is converted into action. (James 1:22-25)

It is not easy to put Christian principles into action. It is difficult to stand for Truth in a world which worships the lie. It can be uncomfortable to follow Jesus.

We can get by without hearing the words of Jesus or without acting upon them. We may be successful at that for a long time and shift with the sands of life as it suits our fancy. However, temporizing weakens our foundations, and ultimately they crumble.

The great poet-preacher John Donne somberly spelled out the consequences of building upon sand.

> We know, O Lord,
> That our rent, due to thee, is our soul;
> And the day of our death is the day,
> And our death-bed the place,
> Where that rent is to be paid.
> And we know too that he that hath sold his soul
> For unjust gain before,
> Or given away his soul before
> In the society of fellowship and sin

Or lent his soul for a time
By lukewarmness and temporizing
To the dishonour of thy name,
To the weakening of thy Cause,
To the discouraging of thy servants,
He comes to that day, and to that place,
His death and death-bed,
Without any rent in his hand,
Without any soul to that purpose,
To surrender it unto thee.

The theme of the parable of the builders is *obedience*. God has a plan for the life of each person. If we are to know what God expects of us, and if we are to fulfill his plan for us, we must listen to and act upon the words of Jesus. We must be obedient. Only then do we build upon the solid rock foundation that will withstand the winds and floods of life.

Check the passages of Scripture referred to above. Summarize each briefly, and then answer the applicable question.

Proverbs 10:25

Summary:

Give an example of the truth of this passage from your own experience.

John 15:1-4

Summary:

How can you tell if you are a branch of the true vine?

John 8:31-32

Summary:

What are some of the freeing effects of living within Christ's revelation?

I Corinthians 3:11

Summary:

What steps are you taking to build upon the foundation that is Christ?

James 1:22-25

Summary:

Give a recent example of doing the Word of God in your own life.

For reflection: What do you think is God's plan for your life (or, if you don't know, what will you do to seek it)?

THE HOLY WAY

Our Lord did not choose a cross
Just because it was a cross.
He did not avoid a pleasure
Just because it was a pleasure.
He followed the way
Of the Holy Will of his Father,

Because it was the Father's will
And the Holy Way.
He never swerved one hair's breadth from it
Either to gain a comfort
Or to avoid a cross.
Things had their value for him
Not because they were sacrifices
But because they were brought to him
By his vocation.

5

Compensation

As is true of most people, I have held a number of jobs in my lifetime. They have ranged from what used to be called a "soda jerk" in a drugstore to the vice-president of a chemical company, then to a variety of positions in Christian work.

For the most part, I have enjoyed them all, and in none of the positions have I been overly concerned about my salary.

There have been times, of course, when I agonized momentarily over whether I was getting a suitable salary for the job I was doing. Like anyone else, I didn't like to be made a fool of, and I wanted to be sure that my compensation was proper for my task.

I once had the opportunity to observe my own reaction to the "proper compensation" game. I didn't like what I saw.

In the several fields in which I have worked, I have been engaged for the most part in administrative work. In this capacity, I frequently have been the contact between the employer and management consultants hired by my company. Management consultants can make an organization uneasy, for employees fear they will recommend drastic changes which will eliminate jobs. Since I was the fellow working with the consultants, I was seldom bothered with this apprehension.

One day, however, the consultants had an unexpected recommendation. They decided that, in relation to my salary, one of my co-workers was underpaid. Moreover, they recommended that he should be making at least as much as I and perhaps more. I was shocked! What could their reasoning possibly be? I was furious.

Fortunately, by God's grace and before things got out of hand, I was able to put things into perspective. Why should it matter to me that a fellow worker was going to receive more pay? It wouldn't cost me anything but my pride, and I could well afford to learn some humility.

Read Matthew 20:1-16. The parable is about God and his grace. (Ephesians 2:8-10) He looks always for laborers for his vineyard. (Matthew 9:37-38) When he has found a few to do his will, he doesn't stop looking. He keeps a constant vigil to win all souls to himself, people of all ages and at all times in their lives. (John 4:35-36) Those who respond he puts into appropriate service.

It is not because of our own efforts that we come into the Kingdom of Heaven. We do not establish a claim there and bargain for our rights. The larger share does not go automatically to the one who labors harder and longer. (Philippians 2:14-18)

God's grace is offered generously to all people. It is his gift. Whether or not it becomes ours depends upon our willingness to accept it and the obligations it entails. We should focus not upon our rights, but upon God's glory and generosity to all his people. (Romans 10:11-12)

The theme of this parable is *attitude*. What counts is not our effort but our attitude, the spirit in which we do what he calls us to do. We can be happy in his Kingdom only when our attitude is one of service to God.

Check the passages of Scripture referred to above. Summarize each briefly, and then answer the applicable question.

Ephesians 2:8-10

Summary:

Give an instance of your receiving grace in the last few days:

Matthew 9:37-38

Summary:

Is there someone to whom God is calling you to go as a "laborer"?

John 4:35-36

Summary:

Are you a sower or a reaper? Explain:

Philippians 2:14-18

Summary:

Have you complained about the way God uses you and were you justified in doing so?

Romans 10:11-12

Summary:

Have you erected barriers between God and someone you don't think he can reach? If so, what will you do about it?

For reflection: What does the parable tell you about what your attitude should be?

UNFULFILMENT

Our prayer must be
That we express what God
Meant each of us to express.
Our penitence must be
That we do not.
Our longing must be
That we may.

Section II

Paul's Letter to Us

Introduction

Scholars believe that Paul wrote the Epistle to the Galatians between 49 and 52 A.D. He composed it hurriedly and under some pressure, much as letters of importance are often written today. Reports had reached Paul that some members of the church were misleading it, and Paul makes an impassioned response. The things Paul said to the Galatians are the same things we in the church need to hear today.

Paul's letter, as you will read it in this study, has been prepared as a letter to us, Christians in the late 20th century. In order that we might get the most out of what he has to say without reference to commentaries explaining each major point and each ambiguous statement, commentary has been incorporated into the text itself.

This is no scholarly work by an experienced Bible scholar, but a labor of love aimed at giving us a unique method of study and perhaps a clearer picture of what Paul was trying to say to a handful of Galatians, and, by the grace of God, to Christians forever. I used many commentaries in putting this study together, always seeking a consensus on any serious issue.

As you read the letter in the form set forth here, consider it to be a letter to the church today, a letter to you as a believing Christian. There are discussion questions at the end of each chapter for individual or group use. If the study is undertaken by a group, it is recommended that one chapter be studied each session, thus providing six sessions of study.

6

Galatians 1

Dear Brothers and Sisters in Christ:

I write you about matters of the gravest concern.

First of all, let there be no doubt about my authority to deal with you on these matters. There are apparently those who would try to convince you that you need not listen to me because I was not one of the original twelve apostles; and indeed, had been an enemy of the early followers of Christ. My authority comes from no human source but by the direct action of God the Father and his son, Jesus Christ, who revealed himself to me on the road to Damascus, commissioned me, and sends me out in his power.

Our Christian fellowship here sends grace and peace to you Christian congregations in Galatia. I am not unmindful of the fact that my preaching among you has drawn you together as a diverse group of people—converts from Judaism, Greek-speaking Gentiles, former slaves in exile from your own homeland, and others. Nonetheless, we are now one in the fellowship of our Lord Jesus Christ, who gave himself to rescue us from sin, in accordance with the will of our God and Father, to whom we give glory forever.

The problem is that some among you are turning you from the gospel of free grace which I preached to you. No one can ever earn the love of God by what he does, particularly by following certain rules and regulations. We give ourselves to God as an act of faith, and it is by that faith in Jesus Christ that we are saved. Is that gospel too simple for you that you must complicate it by imposing the Jewish ritual of circumcision upon those uncircumcised who would follow Christ? I say to you, "Remove from your midst those who would so mislead you!"

Now, some of you will say that I am choosing sides, seeking favor with those who agree with my position and eliminating my opposition by telling you to banish the others. Let me assure you that I would take the same position even if it alienated all of you from me. I am of no value to God if I would sacrifice my principles. I serve him only by stating the truth.

What qualifies me to tell you what the truth is? Because the truth has been revealed directly to me by God and because I am, myself, a living example of how God's grace can turn a person completely around from living by rules and regulations to living by faith.

The gospel I preached to you was not something I learned from someone else. It was a direct revelation from Jesus Christ. Christ called me into his service on the road to Damascus, sent me to Arabia for a time and then back to Damascus. He did not even send me to confer with or learn from those in Jerusalem who were apostles before me.

Furthermore, when Christ called me to be his servant, I was persecuting his church. I, more than many of my Jewish contemporaries, was zealous to the extreme in obeying the Law, the traditions of my ancestors. Yet God had chosen me before I was born to preach his truth among the Gentiles. Look at me! How could one so devoted to the rules and regulations of the Jewish faith be so free of those traditions? Only by the grace of God!

It was three years later before I went to Jerusalem to see Peter for a couple of weeks. The only other apostle I saw at that time was James, the Lord's brother. As God is my judge, those are the plain facts.

I went to Syria and Cilicia, but remained unknown to the Christian churches of Judea. They only heard of me from others, that the former persecutor of the faith was now preaching that faith, which, of course, caused them to glorify God.

DISCUSSION QUESTIONS

1. Paul begins by demonstrating the basis of his authority. How do people try to show the source of their authority today, in and out of the church? What is the best way to demonstrate authority?

2. What is Paul trying to tell us about the nature of the grace to God? Does the church need to hear that message today? Do you?

3. Paul seems to want us to banish from our fellowship those who teach falsely. Is that sound advice today? How could we handle that, in love?

4. Would Paul have won you over to his side on the basis of his argument thus far? Why or why not?

7

Galatians 2

Fourteen years later, Barnabas, Titus, and I went to Jerusalem. God specifically revealed to me that I should go. The situation I faced was not an easy one. I was to make clear to them that my mission to the Gentiles was simply the faith delivered to the church, not something heretical or divisive. I had to walk that narrow path between sticking to my principles yet not alienating the leaders of the church. I wanted their support, that the work I was doing among the Gentiles might not be in vain; but my purpose was more to reveal to them the validity of what I was preaching and doing than to gain support as such.

The question of circumcision was one that had to be met head on. Titus, who was with me, is a Greek and uncircumcised. Pressure from Judaizers [Jewish Christians who mistakenly want to impose Jewish Law upon non-Jewish Christians] caused the church leaders to suggest that (for peace's sake) Titus be circumcised. Titus was, therefore, a test case; and it was clear to me that this was not a point on which to compromise. To have done so would have been to give validity to the bondage of external things to the detriment of the freedom we have in Christ. I stood firm on this, and it was agreed that Titus need not be circumcised.

Those with whom we met (the acknowledged leaders of the church, by position rather than by superiority because, with God, no man is superior to another in the sense of being more important to him) agreed that I had been entrusted with the Gospel to the Gentiles just as Peter had been entrusted with the Gospel to the Jews: that it was, in fact, the same Gospel, that our commissioning by God was equally valid, and that the results of our work likewise showed that God's favor rested upon us. Those recognized as the pillars of the church—the Apostle Peter, the Apostle John, and James, the brother of Jesus—accepted Barnabas and me as partners, and shook hands on it, agreeing that we should go to the Gentiles and they to the Jews. Their sole request was of a practical nature, not a theological one, namely that we have in mind their poor, a concern to which I have responded eagerly.

Later, however, Peter came to Antioch. In Jerusalem, when we had dealt with the matter of circumcision, Peter was removed from the practical implications of the mission to the Gentiles. Now, in Antioch [a much more cosmopolitan city with a church composed of many Gentiles in addition to Jewish Christians], he was confronted with the issue face to face. Initially, he ate with the uncircumcised Christians; but when some people from the church in Jerusalem arrived, Peter withdrew from eating with the Gentiles. The other Jewish Christians did likewise, including even Barnabas! By this action, Peter was clearly wrong and I told him so before the entire congregation.

Such conduct is simply not in accord with the direction that leads to the truth of the Gospel. "You shared fully with the Gentiles," I told Peter, "eating and living as one of them, acknowledging that there is one way for Jew and Gentile alike. Now you are trying to reverse that decision. Now you want to impose circumcision and the Jewish Law upon the Gentiles so as to make them Jews."

We who are Jews by birth have certain privileges; we have moral standards and, in that sense, know right from wrong. The Gentiles are lacking this. Yet, we have learned long ago that no matter how meticulously we attempt to obey the Law, it cannot make us right with God. Scripture tells us that no person can be justified by obeying the Law. The very fact that we know right from wrong, instead of bringing us security, produces anxiety and frustration. Those of us Jews who have become Christians have done so because we realize that it is only through faith in Jesus Christ [the Messiah toward whom the Jews have looked as the key to their history] that we can have a right relationship with God. It is complete dependence upon the love of God in Jesus Christ that gives us freedom from the Law, and makes the Law irrelevant.

It might be argued that ignoring the Jewish Law, and all the good things [moral distinctions that produce noble character and lead to human dignity] that go with it, makes us transgressors of the Law, and Christ a conspirator in that transgression. Freedom in Christ might be all right for those who have moral standards, but what about the Gentiles who have no background in these things? Don't they really need the Jewish Law to teach them obedience and discipline? Such an argument is absurd! It is like trying to build up a new wall that Christ, by showing us a better way, has already torn down. Christ did not tell us to earn salvation by obeying a set of rules and regulations; he told us to throw ourselves unreservedly upon the grace of God. We cannot expect Jewish Christians to live by a set of rules which the Law imposes and the Gentile Christians to be free from those rules; nor can we impose those rules upon the Gentile Christians when we ourselves know that that won't bring salvation but only guilt and frustration. The answer is for us all to live in the freedom which Christ has shown us, dependent solely upon the grace of God.

The Law condemned me to death. Realizing that, I abandoned the way of the Law and cast myself, sinner that I was, on the mercy of God. The Law and my helplessness in trying to fulfill it drew me to God. The resulting change that has been wrought in my life I can only describe by saying that I have been crucified with Christ, and the man I used to be is dead. Accordingly, the life

I now live is Christ living within me. If I could have been in a right relationship with God by obeying the Law, what would have been the need of grace, of the unmerited love and forgiveness which God has shown unto me? If I could have won my own salvation, Christ died for nothing.

DISCUSSION QUESTIONS

1. In Galatians 1, Paul sounded like someone unwilling to compromise. In the first part of Galatians 2, however, he talks about being careful not to alienate the leaders of the church. Is a difference in attitude reflected here; and, if so, was it justified?

2. How do you feel about Peter, based upon what Paul says he did in Antioch? Is this reminiscent of Peter before Jesus' crucifixion? Does the church vacillate on other matters today? Do you?

3. What, according to Paul, were the advantages to the Law? Are there advantages to rules and regulations in the church today? Give some examples.

4. What, at this point, do you understand Paul to be saying about the purpose and the limitations of the Law?

8

Galatians 3

Poor misled people! What are you thinking? It is as though an evil spell has been cast upon you. Are you the same people before whom I so clearly showed Christ crucified?

With my own eyes I have seen the Holy Spirit manifested among you. There came to you life and power which anyone could see. Did the Spirit come to you because you followed the Jewish Law or because you listened to the Gospel and believed? Have you missed the point of why you have experienced these demonstrations of God's love? Do you not know why God, through his Holy Spirit, has performed miracles among you? Do you think it is because you keep the Law, or is it because you have faith in Christ?

Perhaps the clearest way to see the principle I am trying to show you is to demonstrate it in the life of Abraham. Abraham put his faith in God and became a man who pleased God.

What, then, is the identifying characteristic of Abraham—his Jewishness or his faith? I say it is his faith. Therefore, the true descendants of Abraham, and the heirs to the blessings which God laid upon him and his descendants, are not those who, by chance of birth, are of his bloodline, but those who have the faith of Abraham.

If you decide to try to win God's favor by accepting and obeying the Law, what are the inescapable conclusions to which you are led? First, you must stand or fall on that decision; if you choose to follow the Law, you are bound by the precepts of the Law. Second, you have established a goal that cannot be reached; no one will ever be able fully to obey the Law. Third, if my conclusions thus far are correct, you are putting yourself under a curse because Deuteronomy 27:26 says that unless you keep the whole Law you are under a curse. Thus, the inescapable conclusion of attempting to gain a right relationship with God by making the Law the principle of your life is simply to put yourself under a curse.

On the other hand, Habakkuk 2:4 says that the just shall live by faith. Therefore, the only way to be in harmony with God's purposes for your life, and to experience the resulting peace of God, is the way of faith.

Furthermore, the two principles—the way of the Law and the way of faith—are incompatible. You cannot live your life according to both of them at the same time. The choice is yours, and the only sensible choice is to forgo the way of the Law and to seize upon the way of faith.

How can this be so? Because of what Jesus Christ did for us all. Through the cross, Christ identified himself with everyone whom the Law condemns. Deuteronomy 21:23 says that he who is crucified (hanged upon a tree) is accursed of God. Christ, by his crucifixion, became accursed by the Law to release us from the Law's curse. Jesus became accursed to show us how much God loves us. Through Christ, the blessings of Abraham have been extended to all that all may live by grace who live by faith.

Now, let us consider another illustration. I will do this in the manner of a trained rabbi, using a method of argument that will be more meaningful to some of you [the Jewish Christians] than to others.

First of all, the way of faith is older than the way of Law.

When Abraham by faith did as God bid him, God made a great promise to him. God's promise was activated by a showing of faith; that is, the foundation of the agreement between God and Abraham was faith. The Law did not come until hundreds of years later, through Moses.

Second, once a covenant of the type that existed between God and Abraham has been made it cannot be amended or repudiated; it must remain unaltered. The Law, which came later, could not change the way of faith. Faith was the basis of the covenant, and is still the only way for a person to have a right relationship with God.

Third, let us look at the word "issue." In Genesis 17:7 and 8, God says to Abraham that he will establish his covenant with Abraham and his issue, or descendant. The word used is in the singular, not the plural. I say that the word was intentionally singular because God meant by "issue" Christ himself.

Thus, the way to a right relationship with God is by faith because the relationship was covenanted between God and Abraham. Further, the coming of the Law hundreds of years later could not invalidate the covenant of faith. And, finally, it is in looking to Jesus Christ that we see the way of perfect faith.

What, then, was the purpose of the Law? The Law exists because evil exists. It is an addition to the original plan, to reveal, restrain and render harmless the effects of evil. Its value is an expedient means of dealing with a particular—though serious and universal—problem. The strength of the Law is that it helps us to understand sin; its weakness is that it does nothing to alleviate sin.

(Furthermore, it is my contention that the Law was not given directly by God as the promise to Abraham had been. I believe that the Law was given by angels, through Moses as an intermediary, to the people. Therefore, I simply do not believe that the Law has the same standing as the covenant with Abraham.)

If, then, as I have said earlier, the way of the Law and the way of faith are incompatible, is the Law contrary to the promises of God? Absolutely not! The Law has a very useful purpose when properly understood. The Law (Deuteronomy 27:26) has put everyone under subjection to sin [it has shown us what sin is]. The consequence of the Law is that it shows us our helplessness and drives us to seek God's grace which is available to us through faith in Jesus Christ.

Before Christ came we were prisoners in the custody of the Law, awaiting the full revelation of faith. We were like the privileged child who is in the charge of a custodian of his moral welfare. In our day families of means provide old and trusted slaves to take care of their children, protecting them from temptations and dangers, and leading them toward maturity as people. That was the function of the Law. It could bring us to a certain point. It could take care of us until Christ came. It could lead us to Christ; but it could not take us into a relationship with him. When faith comes, we no longer need the custodian. Faith is the real maturity at which God would have us arrive. The mature person is not only knowledgeable, wise, and experienced—he is receptive. He is capable of being surprised. Faith is the capacity to be surprised by God—by what God is and by what he gives.

Where does that leave us who have accepted Jesus Christ in faith? We are now truly sons of God! Through baptism, we are at one with Christ himself. It is as though we have taken off the clothes of our old life and been clothed anew with the garments of Christ's righteousness. It no longer matters whether we are Jew or Greek, slave or free, male or female. The differences between human beings are no longer of any significance; these distinctions are destroyed in favor of complete equality within union in Christ. Furthermore, by belonging to Christ, the true issue [decendant] of Abraham, we are heirs of the promise of God's grace-filled blessings.

DISCUSSION QUESTIONS

1. After chastising us, Paul says that he had seen the Holy Spirit manifested among us. In what ways would the presence and power of the Holy Spirit be evident among us today?

2. What, in your opinion, are the strong points and weak points in Paul's argument about the distinction between the Law and faith?

3. What is now your understanding of Paul's teaching concerning the purpose and limitations of the Law?

4. Paul seems to say that a mature person is one who is receptive and capable of being surprised, and that faith is the capacity to be surprised by God. Discuss the nature of faith.

9

Galatians 4

Let me draw yet another analogy. Although a person may be the heir of a large estate, while he is still a minor he is no better off than a slave insofar as possessing the proceeds of that estate is concerned. He may technically be the owner of the property, but he can make no legally binding decision until he comes of age. In this sense he has no more freedom than a slave until he reaches the designated age when he can come into his full inheritance and the freedom of manhood.

In a way, that is how things have been in the world. During the "childhood" of the world, we were ruled by the Law, elementary knowledge though it was. We were concerned with doing basic things in a set pattern, like helpless children living under the oppression of the Law. But, in the fullness of time, when God determined that the world's period of basic training was over, he sent his own Son to release us from the tyranny of the Law. That Son, Jesus Christ, was born of a woman and was born under the Law—the same conditions under which you and I were born—in order to buy our freedom from the oppression of the Law, that we all—Jews and Gentiles alike—might attain the status of sons of God.

In former times, before you put your faith in Christ, some of you were ruled by elementary knowledge carried out in a systematic way [the Law] while others were under the power of ungodly spirits [astrology and mythology]. You were, in fact, slaves. Now that God has claimed you as his own, why do you revert to your former slavish ways? By making a fetish of certain days and times of the year, and attaching undue significance to them, you are returning to legalistic religious play-acting. Has all that I have suffered for your sake simply been in vain?

Wait a minute. I'm tired of arguing. Let me appeal to you as your brother. For your sake, I became as a Gentile, abandoning the traditions of my upbringing. I ask now that you become as I am, free of the Law.

I originally came to you as a sick man. You could have rejected me. On the contrary, you accepted me as you would have accepted Christ himself. You would have given me your own eyes. You could not have been nicer to me, and I am grateful for that. But now, have I become your enemy because I'm being frank with you?

The Judaizers among you are up to no good. They are playing up to you that they may win you over to their point of view, so that you will adopt their Jewish ways. Then you will have to play up to them in order to comply with their doctrines!

My dear children, I wish I could be with you now. I am like a mother in the travail of birth over you. It is as though I must go through the pains of birth with you once again in order for you to be born in Christ. If I were with you, perhaps I wouldn't have to talk to you so sternly. But, in truth, you have me at my wits' end.

Because you take the Law so seriously, let us listen to what the Law says. It is written in the Law that Abraham had two sons. One was born of Hagar, his wife Sarah's slave. Because she was barren, Sarah had hoped to give Abraham offspring in this second-handed way. In the meantime, however, God had made a promise to Abraham that he would have a son by Sarah. The son born to Hagar was Ishmael; the son born to Sarah was Isaac. Ishmael mocked Isaac; and Sarah insisted that Hagar and Ishmael be cast out, for the child of a slave girl should not share in the inheritance of the legitimate heir.

Speaking again in the manner of a trained rabbi, I ask you to look at this story as an allegory. The two women represent the two covenants. Hagar represents Judaism and the covenant of the Law. Sarah represents the covenant of faith (promise) and freedom from the Law. Hagar represents slavery, Sarah freedom. Sarah is our mother, and we are not under the yoke of Judaism, but under the freedom of the spiritual Jerusalem, God's heavenly kingdom, a community of children of the promise [faith]. (Isaiah 54:1).

You, my sisters and brothers, are children of the promise, as Isaac was. Isaac was presecuted [mocked] by Ishmael, and so it is today. But what does Scripture say? "Cast out this handwoman and her son; for the son of this handwoman shall not be heir with my son, even with Isaac" (Gen. 21:10). We, my sisters and brothers, are children of the free woman, not the slave. The slave must spend all of his life trying to satisfy the Law, but we live by love and not by Law. Stand firm in your freedom: do not allow yourselves to be put under the yoke of slavery.

DISCUSSION QUESTIONS

1. Paul talks about Christ coming in the fullness of time, at the moment in the history of the world when all had been adequately prepared for this gift of all gifts. Christ has, in fact, been called "the hinge of history." What do you think about that?

2. Paul says that the proof of our sonship (as heirs of God) is the inner relevation of the Holy Spirit. Discuss.

3. Having engaged in several technical arguments Paul then "shifts gears" and appeals to us as a friend. Is argument the most effective way of winning a person over to Christ or to a point of view concerning faith? If not, what is?

4. Paul concludes the chapter with another argument, this one involving Sarah/Isaac and Hagar/Ishmael. In what ways is his analogy helpful to you?

10

Galatians 5

Listen carefully: This is Paul speaking to you. The way of the Law and the way of faith are incompatible. The way of the Law assumes that we can, by our own action, win favor with God. The way of faith recognizes that we must throw ourselves and our sin upon the mercy of God. Therefore, if you decide that a man must be circumcised, you are accepting the way of the Law and denying the way of faith. Christ, then, is of no avail to you. By recognizing one part of the Law, you become obligated to all of it. In seeking to be justified by the Law, you are abandoning the way of faith, and you are cutting yourself off from Christ who died to free you from the Law. To be in a right relationship with God is not something we can achieve, but only something we can receive as a gift from God, by faith through his Holy Spirit. The key is not the Law but a personal relationship with Jesus Christ. If we have that relationship, circumcision is pointless. The only thing that matters is faith manifested by love.

You were getting along just fine. What caused you to get off the track? What obstacle stopped you from following the truth? A bad apple can spoil the whole barrel, and the "bad apple" among you did not come from God. The attraction to legalism among you needs to be gotten rid of before it pollutes

53

you, and I am confident that you will do the right thing. The person who is unsettling your minds must face the judgment of God. As for me, let it be clear that I do not preach circumcision but the cross as the only way of coming into a right relationship with God.

Heathen priests mutilated themselves by castration. For those who would argue for circumcision, let them go ahead and castrate themselves!

Now let's consider the practical applications of what we have been talking about. You should have a clear understanding of what I mean by freedom. There is a difference between freedom and license. True freedom implies service to others. If, by our "freedom," we take advantage of, or do not give due consideration to, others, then we have limited their freedom. Thus, as free people, we are called to God to love one another as ourselves. (If you do the opposite, you will destroy yourselves.)

Be guided by the Holy Spirit of God and not by the desires of your lower nature. The desires of the lower side of human nature are at enmity with the desires of the Holy Spirit. Thus you must yield to the inner promptings of the Spirit and be led by them in order to overcome the desires of your lower nature. (Likewise, life under guidance of the Holy Spirit is a life of faith and love rather than a life under the Law [legalistic obedience], which, for reasons already stated, cannot bring ultimate fulfillment.)

You surely know what I mean by the thoughts and deeds of the lower nature, but I will list some of them to be sure you understand: fornication [sexual intercourse by an unmarried person], impurity [that which makes a person unfit or unclean to come before God], and wantonness [so lustful as to not care what others think]; idolatry [letting things made by man take the place of God] and sorcery [witchcraft]; hatred, strife [quarreling and wrangling], envy, fits of rage, selfish ambitions, dissension, divisiveness, and jealousy; drunkenness, carousing, and such things. As I have warned you before, people who behave in these ways are not living in the Kingdom of God.

On the other hand, the fruit of the Holy Spirit of God is love [seeking the best for others], joy [being in a right relationship with God], peace [all-pervading consciousness that our time is in the hands of God], patience [forbearance], kindness [a character trait that reveals an understanding of the fragile nature of human personality], goodness [righteousness softened by love], fidelity [trustworthiness], gentleness [consideration toward others], and self-control [self-discipline]. Such things do not result from the Law, and against them the Law is impotent and irrelevant; they simply have nothing to do with the Law. The lower nature, with its desires and ambitions, has been crucified with Christ in those who choose to live by the Spirit; and those who have come alive through the Spirit of God within them should let the Spirit guide their way. Therefore, conceit, rivalry and envy should have no place with you.

DISCUSSION QUESTIONS

1. Paul takes one more parting shot at the distinction between the Law and faith. Here he comes down hard on the need for a relationship with God, with Christ, through faith. Discuss what it means to have a personal relationship with God.

2. Paul next draws an important distinction between freedom and license. Do you agree with the definition of "true freedom"?

3. Next, Paul discusses the thoughts and deeds of our lower nature, and names several of them just to be sure we know what he is talking about. Do you agree with his list? Why or why not?

4. On a positive note, we then are told about the fruit of the Spirit. In what ways have you seen such fruit manifested in your own life, not because of your innate goodness, tact, or talent but because of God's Spirit working within you?

11

Galatians 6

Dear people, if someone slips and falls into some immoral act, those of you who are guided by the Spirit of God have a responsibility to confront the person, but with gentleness. And remember, you may be tempted, too; so don't think too highly of yourself. Carry one another's burdens to fulfill Christ's commandment that you love one another as you love yourself.

Don't be deceived concerning your own importance. Don't compare your accomplishments with anyone else's but with what you could have done if you had done your best. Carry your own share of the load.

Concerning Christian teachers, support them. If someone is using his or her time and talent to teach you eternal truths, then you have an obligation to share with him the material things that you have gained from the use of your own time and talent.

And make no mistake about this: God cannot be fooled; whatever one sows one will also reap. If one plants a crop in his lower nature [engages in fleshly indulgences], he will reap a bitter harvest. But he who plants his crop in the field of God's Holy Spirit [devotes his life to doing the will of God] will reap eternal life. So don't give up on doing what God calls you to do; persevere, and God will reward your efforts. As opportunities present themselves, work for the good of all, especially fellow Christians.

I conclude by writing in my own hand and in bold letters that you may know how seriously I regard this message to you. Those who want to satisfy their own desire for recognition are trying to force circumcision upon you. Their real purpose is to avoid looking solely to the cross of Christ as their means of coming into a saving relationship with Jesus Christ. These people are interested in externals. But God forbid that I should boast of anything but the cross of our Lord Jesus Christ, through which the world of which I was previously a part has been crucified to me [is no longer a part of me] and I to the world! My life has been revolutionized in Christ. Neither circumcision nor uncircumcision means a thing; the only thing that matters is to be a new creation, the spiritual re-creation of the person in Christ Jesus. May God bless and guide all who live by this principle, for they are the real Israel, the true heirs of Abraham.

The marks of Christ branded on my body are sufficient evidence of my devotion to him.

May the grace of our Lord Jesus Christ be with your spirit, my brothers and sisters. Amen.

DISCUSSION QUESTIONS

1. Paul now gives some practical advice. He begins by telling us to confront those of our fellowship who fall into immoral acts, but to do it with gentleness. Is that possible in the church today? How?

2. We are told to support Christian teachers. Is that part of the plan of the church of today? In what way?

3. God will not be fooled, Paul tells us. How, then, are we to live? Is Paul's guidance of practical help to you? Explain.

4. Paul bears the marks of Christ. How may we?

Section III

Setting Christ Free

Introduction

One of the best-selling Christian classics of all times is *In His Steps* by Charles Sheldon. Simply stated, it is a story of people who tried to make every decision by asking themselves the question, "What would Christ do in this situation?"

By the power of the Holy Spirit, Christ lives within his people. He is within us to guide us, to help us know "what he would do." The problem is that we often tend to go our own way rather than realizing the Christ within us that we might be—as we are called to be—Christ in the world.

This study looks at eight characteristics of Christ as they are manifested in the Gospels. With regard to each characteristic, we are to explore how we might free Christ within us that that attribute might be manifested in our lives.

There are eight chapters in "Setting Christ Free," so eight sessions of study are possible with this material.

12

The Authority of Christ

At luncheon time a new friend commented on needs that are going unmet. "It is disheartening," she said, "that so many people who are under psychiatric care could be getting help through their churches and don't even know it. Worse still, there are countless people who don't even think the church is relevant to their needs."

"The primary reason for that," I replied "is the weakness of the church's witness. A person under psychiatric care, or facing similar needs, looks at his Christian friend and says, 'He's got the same problems I do, and I don't see the church helping him.' The church today doesn't speak with enough authority to command the attention of the world around it, nor to convince many people that it has answers to their needs."

When Jesus spoke; however, people listened. People were astounded at his teaching because he spoke with a note of authority, unlike the other Jewish teachers of the day (Matthew 7:29). Through his actions, such as when unclean spirits submitted to him, they saw his authority demonstrated (Mark 1:21-28). In giving his followers the "Great Commission," Jesus claimed the authority granted unto him to send them forth (Matthew 28:18).

Christ's authority remains in his church today, and resides in individual Christians. It is as we allow that authority to be manifested through us that the world will see that the church does have answers to the world's needs. Churches are to be hospitals, not museums; Christians are to be instruments of God's healing power, not curators of history.

For the authority of Christ to be freed from within us, there are at least four prerequisites that must be met: (1) we are in a right relationship with God, (2) we are in a right relationship with our neighbor, (3) we know the authority from which we speak, and (4) our actions are authenticated by the ways in which God has equipped us.

The first prerequisite is so obvious as to need little explanation. Jesus maintained a close and constant relationship with the Father, allowing authority to flow to him unimpeded. We, likewise, must have a close relationship with God if his authority is to be manifested in us. If we are in a state of disobedience or apathy, the flow of authority is impaired.

A wrong relationship with a fellow human being will also impede the release of Christ's authority within us. That is because, if we are not reconciled to our brother, we are not in a right relationship with God. "If, when you are bringing your gift to the altar," Jesus said, "you suddenly remember that your brother has a grievance against you, leave your gift where it is before the altar. First go and make your peace with your brother, and only then come back and offer your gift." (Matthew 5:23-24).

If we are to speak with Christ's authority, we must also be rooted in that authority as revealed in Scripture. When Jesus was tempted by Satan in the wilderness (Luke 4:1-13), he did not engage in intellectual debate; he stood on the authority of Scripture. We are called to be growing in our understanding of Scripture that we may better know, day by day, the authority upon which we are to stand.

Finally, our authority is dependent upon the gifts God has given us and on the ways he has equipped us to do his will. Our authority will be Christ's authority as it is dependent upon the spiritual gifts we have been given for ministry. A person who has been gifted by God for a healing ministry, for instance, will show forth Christ's authority in a healing situation more effectively than someone whose gift is evangelism.

Likewise, God equips us for Christ's ministry in the world in many other ways—through our talents, vocations, skills, education, and our peculiar experiences in life if we can see that life is God's training ground for us. Then our actions are authenticated by the base of training from which we proceed. We come across as people who know whereof we speak because God has taught us in the school of life.

If we, as Christians, would maintain a right relationship with God and our neighbor, would engage in a regular program of Bible study, and would rely upon the gifts and other "equipping" God has given us for ministry, we could release the authority of Christ within us. We could free the Christ in us to speak with authority and conviction; and the world would pay attention, as it did to Christ himself.

A few years ago I was faced with the opportunity of making a vocational change. Because of the seriousness of the situation and the lack of clear guidance as to what I should do, I sought counsel from a Christian friend. He suggested that my wife and I go away for three days of fasting and prayer.

"There is no way I can do that anytime soon," I protested, "there are simply too many other things on my schedule right now." My friend did not back down an inch. "What if your wife were suddenly seriously ill?" he asked. "Would you be too busy to care for her?"

"Of course not," I replied. Then, speaking with the authority of Christ, my friend said, "The decision you must make about your vocation is of similar importance; set aside three days for fasting and prayer immediately." I did, and it led to my making the job change into the extremely fulfilling ministry in which I am now engaged.

If my friend had not spoken with the authority of Christ, I am not sure that I would have given that vocational change the consideration that is so justly deserved.

QUESTIONS

1. Give an example from your own experience of having "paid
   attention" to what someone said or did because you knew it
   was with the authority of Christ.

2. Give an example of Christ's authority being manifested through
   your own life.

3. What is the primary thing impeding you from releasing Christ's
   authority within you?

4. What is your plan to remove that impediment?

13

The Compassion of Christ

Our friend Don cries so often that his nickname is "Weepy." Don is a "man's man"; there is certainly nothing sissy about him. Yet at the slightest provocation—someone in need, a tragic story, or even a victory achieved—Don's eyes will begin to tear up.

He came by my office one time to ask for my prayers as he went into a counseling session. Counseling is the ministry to which he has been called as a lay person, and he spends many hours helping others in that way.

We had a brief visit during which he told me of a letter he had received earlier in the day. It was from a young woman Don had felt prompted to call concerning a problem he knew she was working through. The letter was to thank Don for his timely call and for the ways in which he had helped her. His eyes began to moisten as he thanked God for using him in that special way.

Jesus, of course, had a similar problem. He is our example of what compassion is all about. The Bible says his heart went out to people with need he saw around him (Matthew 14:13-14; Luke 7:11-17).

The elements of compassion that Jesus demonstrated were at least fourfold. (1) He *was not superficial* in his compassion. (2) It *covered a wide range* of situations. (3) Jesus *did not hide* his compassion. (4) He *did something* about the concerns he felt.

The emotions which Christ expressed were real ones. As he went from town to town teaching and healing, "the sight of the people moved him to pity" as we see in Matthew 9:35-38. "They were like sheep without a shepherd, harassed and helpless." Jesus saw people as they really are, and his heart ached for them.

We must be careful, if we are to allow Christ's compassion to flow through us, that we not be superficial in our concern. It hurts to hurt for others, so we often protect ourselves by contributing money out of our abundance and letting that substitute for personal concern. My friend Don works "one on one" as Jesus did, in situations in which the fraud of superficiality is impossible.

There was a breadth of compassion demonstrated by Christ which also should be a lesson to us. It ran from the ultimate concerns of God to the grief of losing a friend.

Jesus's compassion for Jerusalem (Matthew 23:37-39) demonstrates how attuned he was to God's will for the Jews, and how deeply he hurt because of their blindness.

> O Jerusalem, Jerusalem, the city that murders the prophets and stones the messengers sent to her! How often have I longed to gather your children, as a hen gathers her brood under her wings; but you would not let me. Look, look! there is your temple, forsaken by God. And I tell you, you shall never see me until the time when you say, "Blessings on him who comes in the name of the Lord."

Yet Christ's compassion was also as natural as the heartbreak of anyone who has lost a friend (John 11:32-36).

We aren't meant to compartmentalize our compassion. It is easy to care about those whom we love deeply, but Jesus cared with his Father's care, and that reached from Lazarus to the lost sheep of the house of Israel. God wants us to care with that breadth of caring.

The Lazarus story (John 11:32-36) also shows us that Christ did not hide his compassion. He wasn't afraid to weep. There is great healing power in releasing our tears, and we free the Christ within us when we weep tears of compassion—because they are his tears.

Finally, the Bible shows us that Jesus did something about the concerns around him. He took action to help those in need. He did everything from feeding them (Matthew 15:32-37) to healing them (Matthew 20:29-34).

Although it is appropriate to cry as a means of releasing our compassion, our concern shouldn't stop there. Weeping alone can be a dead-end street, particularly if, for instance, we are feeling sorry for ourselves concerning the loss of a loved one. God calls us to action through the compassion of Christ he has placed in our hearts.

If we would allow Christ's compassion to flow through us to meet the needs of a very needful world around us, Jesus has given us some helpful guidelines. We must deal with our superficiality, to ensure that our concern is real. We should likewise not be too selective about our caring, limiting it to our selfish concerns. We should be free to show our compassion, not afraid to weep Christ's tears; and we should be ready to do our share to make things right.

A few years ago I had the pleasure of meeting a widow whom God uses to minister to other widows. I met her at a time when I was devising ways to help people discover the ministries to which God calls them as laypeople. I have no idea what her special gifts for ministry were, other than the tragic experience of the death of her husband.

Here was a woman who had coped, through the grace of God, with the loss of her loved one. Through it she had learned how to help others deal with the identical problem. Christ's compassion flowed freely through her as she ministered in this special way to widows all over the town where she lived.

Someone asked her why she felt competent to help widows though she had had no special training. "Your clergy have had extensive instruction in counseling the bereaved," the person said. "Why should they send you?" "Because," she replied, "they have never lost a husband."

QUESTIONS

1. Give an example from your own experience of someone demonstrating the compassion of Christ.

2. Tell about Christ's compassion being manifested in your own life.

3. What may be keeping you from being a clear channel of Christ's compassion?

4. What is your plan to free the compassionate Christ within you?

14

The Grace of Christ

A friend of mine who is an Episcopal priest had an interesting experience. His secretary was desperately ill, in critical condition for almost a week.

Marie's heart stopped beating on three different occasions, she had been virtually comatose for days; she had been transferred from one hospital to another, and the doctors were baffled by her illness. Through all of this, my friend was sustained in the belief that she was in God's hands, and he had real hope for her recovery.

Then there was a small breakthrough. A kidney specialist made a preliminary determination concerning her ailment and put her on "the kidney machine" with the belief that she would improve. Armed with this good news, my priest friend immediately began calling people he knew should be informed about Marie's condition. When he finished, he felt incomplete. There was someone he had not told, and he couldn't figure out who it was.

It was Marie! For years she has been my friend's "right arm." She had not only shared the workload, but the prayer load of the congregation. She had always been kept fully informed of the things she could be told because her prayer support was so necessary. But it was only when she herself became incapacitated that the sustaining grace she brings to her work/ministry was fully recognized.

God sustains us like that. His love and mercy keep us going much more than we realize. His grace is truly sufficient.

God's grace, reflected in the person of Jesus Christ, is shown often in the Bible. God's grace: (1) *Enhances.* "The child [Jesus] grew big and strong and full of wisdom; and God's favor was upon him." (Luke 2:40). We can only imagine how dynamic a figure Christ must have been, but we know that people immediately noticed him. However those charismatic qualities were reflected in him, it was obvious to those with eyes to see that he was full of grace. (2) *Sustains.* When Paul prayed that the "thorn in the flesh" would be removed, he was told by God: "My grace is all you need; power comes to its full strength in my weakness" (2 Corinthians 12:9). Paul realized that what he did in his own strength was insignificant in comparison to what God could do through him; and he probably also realized that, in his own strength, he would get on some ungodly tangents rather than doing the will of God. He recognized his constant need for the sustaining grace of God. (3) *Forgives.* In his First Letter to Timothy (1:12-13), Paul also realized what God had done for him despite the havoc he had wrought upon the church in his pre-Christian days. "I thank him who made me equal to the task, Jesus Christ our Lord; I thank him for judging me worthy of this trust and appointing me to his service—although in the past I had met him with abuse and persecution and outrage." Paul had been at the forefront of persecution of the church, and God not only forgave him, but put him into the forefront of heading that church. God's grace forgives. (4) *Strengthens.* In his Second Letter to Timothy (2:1), Paul teaches us yet another thing about the grace of God. "Now therefore, my son, take strength from the grace of God which is ours in Christ Jesus." He then gives Timothy a challenging assignment, knowing that the young man can fulfill it despite many obstacles because of the strength he receives by the grace of God.

How can we, through freeing Christ within us, be instruments of God's grace in enhancing, sustaining, forgiving and strengthening?

We live in an age when people are lonely and need to be loved.

It seems that the closer we live together in the concrete jungles of our modern age, the further apart we are. Christ would have us enhance, enrich the lives of others, by pouring his grace through us if we will only take a little time to affirm those with whom we come into contact.

People also need to be encouraged to cope with the pain of life just as Paul wanted help with his "thorn in the flesh." We can bring the sustaining grace of Christ to them if we will only listen to their hurt, pray with them, and let them know that we care.

Christ in us is very quick to forgive. Forgiveness is love in action; not just accepting a person's apology, but trying to make an enemy a friend. Christ turned Paul the persecutor into the champion of the Christian faith. He can also do things like that through us—if we will let him.

The grace of Christ can also flow through us to strengthen those for whom we have responsibility: our spouses, our children, our fellow workers. Those who are close to us need encouragement to go out and do the work that is expected of them. We can give them our best if we allow the Christ within us to strengthen them through his grace.

At a recent meeting of civic and business leaders in our community, a high school girl was the featured speaker. It was the sort of occasion at which a nationally known personality would normally have given the address. No "superstar," however, would ever have been greeted with the thunderous applause that followed the talk by this young girl.

She told how disease had constantly stood in the way of her desire to be a winning athlete in basketball and track at her school; and how, by the grace of God, she had been able to overcome those obstacles time and time again. Now, however, the prognosis was that her condition was terminal (she has since died). But as she stood before that spellbound audience, nothing came from her lips but thankfulness and love.

God's grace had enhanced, sustained, forgiven, and strengthened her, and that grace freely flowed through her as she prepared for the next great step of faith.

QUESTIONS

1. Give an example of God's grace in your life.

2. Give an example of the manifestation of grace in the life of another.

3. How may God use us—by his grace—to encourage and strengthen others?

4. What will you do to be a more effective channel of God's grace?

15

The Intercession of Christ

Sometime ago I heard the story of a young man who had returned home from the Viet Nam war. His parents greeted him with, "We knew you'd come home safely because we prayed for you all the time you were gone."

"Don't tell me about prayer," replied the young man angrily. "I prayed regularly for my best buddy, too, but he got shot to pieces before my very eyes."

There aren't any easy answers when it comes to the matter of effective prayer on behalf of others, what we call intercession. We only know that God expects us to pray for others, and he does use that love-energy to effect good in some way.

Jesus as Intercessor displayed a unique range of prayers on behalf of others. Even back in the Old Testament (Isaiah 53:12) the prophecy concerning the Messiah refers to him as one who "bore the sin of many and interceded for their transgressions."

In his final instructions to his disciples before his betrayal, Jesus tells Peter that he has prayed for him that his faith will not fail (Luke 22:32). On the cross he prays, "Father, forgive them; they do not know what they are doing" (Luke 23:34). Even in those great crises of his life, Jesus takes time to pray for others.

The 17th chapter of the Gospel of John contains Jesus' finest example of intercession. It is one of the most poetically beautiful and profoundly moving passages in literature. In it Jesus literally takes those who have followed him and will follow him in the years to come and wraps them in prayer.

Jesus had already promised (John 14:16) to pray for the Father to send the Holy Spirit to be with his followers.

Finally, as we learn from Romans 8:34 and Hebrews 7:25, Christ is at God's right hand pleading our cause.

Christ enriches us in his prayers. He has gone before us in prayer, preparing the way for us. He has died on a cross, forgiving us. He has sent his Holy Spirit to protect and guide us. And now he is at the Father's right hand pleading on our behalf.

It seems little enough to expect that we should encircle others in prayer. The Christ within us would have us be intercessors that our prayers may be his prayers for others.

In a sense, we can illustrate this process of encircling others in prayer by praying for them (especially our children) before they are even born. Psychology has revealed how much a child lives, learns, and is affected by the time in the womb. A friend of mine has a fine son for whom he prayed regularly while placing his hand on his wife's abdomen during her pregnancy.

We can pray for others in the joys of life as well as the sorrows. Too often we wait until others are in trouble before praying for them. We should, instead, surround others—particularly those for whom God has given us special responsibility—with joyous prayers of thanksgiving for their lives, that their lives may be bountiful in the will of God. God will use the love-energy to bring fulfillment in the lives of those for whom we pray.

But we should also pray for those in pain, or trial, or facing death. We should be prepared to carry their burden with them. We should be willing to pray to exhaustion on behalf of those who suffer. Sometimes, in such instances, God asks us to "put feet on our prayers"; he gives us things to do. At other times we are simply to keep on praying. We will see "results," some of which will seem to be "no" answers to our prayers; but the results aren't as important as the obedience with which we intercede.

As I write these words a good friend of ours is dying. Over

four years ago Louise was diagnosed as having incurable cancer. It was just a matter of time, said the doctors, and a very brief time at that.

Many prayers went up for Louise. She is such a bright spot in the lives of so many that she became encircled in these prayers. As a result, she experienced a miraculous healing and has sustained the rest of us with her joyous Christian spirit over the intervening years.

Recently, however, the cancer returned. No amount of praying seems to be able to stop the ravaging of her body this time. Yet is not now just as important a time as any to free the Christ within us that our prayers may be his prayers as Louise comes into the wholeness that only death can bring—and goes home to be with her Lord?

QUESTIONS

1. For whom do you intercede regularly and why that particular person or persons?

2. What is your method of praying for others?

3. What have been some results of your prayers for others?

4. How can you become a more effective intercessor?

16

The Mystery of Christ

Christians should be "mystery people." They should live within the hope that was so beautifully expressed by J.B. Phillips in his translation of Romans 8:18-19: "In my opinion, whatever we may have to go through now is less than nothing compared with the magnificent future God has planned for us. The whole creation is on tiptoe to see the wonderful sight of the sons of God coming into their own."

Paul had much to say about the mystery of Christ, the secret of eternal life that God revealed to man through Christ. He referred to that "secret" in at least five of his Epistles:

The divine secret (Romans 16:25-27). In his closing of the Epistle, Paul refers to the proclamation of Jesus Christ, "according to the revelation of that divine secret kept in silence for long ages but now disclosed. . . ."

God's hidden wisdom (1 Corinthians 2:7). Here Paul says that the wisdom he speaks is not of the temporal world, but, "I speak God's hidden wisdom, his secret purpose from the very beginning to bring us to our full glory."

God's hidden purpose (Ephesians 1:9-10). "He has made known

to us his hidden purpose—such was his will and pleasure determined before in Christ—to be put into effect when the time was
ripe: namely that the universe, all in heaven and earth, might be
brought to unity in Christ."

The hope of glory (Colossians 1:27). "The secret is this: Christ
in you, the hope of a glory to come."

The mystery of our religion (1 Timothy 3:16). "And great beyond
all question is the mystery of our religion:

> He who was manifested into the body,
> vindicated in the spirit,
> seen by angels;
>> Who was proclaimed among the nations,
>> believed in throughout the world,
>> glorified in high heaven."

What are we to make of all this? Paul is talking of a hope, secret,
mystery, and hidden wisdom which Christians should be carrying
with them wherever they go. It involves knowing deeply within
them the truths that God revealed in Christ.

One aspect of that inner knowledge is realizing that we are
already living eternally. I can still remember very clearly when
the conviction that I am living forever with God came to me. It
was long after I had accepted Christ as my Lord and Savior. It
wasn't as much of a feeling as it was a discovery of truth, and
the assurance and inner peace that comes with that. Regardless
of what happens to me in the days and years ahead, I belong to
God and will dwell with him eternally, and that's pretty good
"mystery" to be carrying around.

Have you ever met a person who reflected so much inner joy
that he looked as though he had swallowed a light bulb? That is
also a result of knowing God's mystery as revealed in Christ. It
is one manifestation of releasing the Christ within us, that we may
freely shine in the world. And it happens because we know the

joy of living in accordance with God's purpose for our life.

Inner peace is another result of understanding God's secret. A man came up to me recently to discuss his neighbor who was not a Christian but a very good and considerate person. "How can I be a witness to him?" he asked. "He seems to be getting along fine without a relationship with God."

"If you are the kind of Christian that I perceive you to be to your neighbor, it will just be a matter of time until you can witness to him," I said. "He is living very well at a superficial level, but one day a problem will come along which he can't handle in his humanness. Then, he will be looking for someone who has inner peace with whom he can talk about his real fears and uncertainties. That is when he will come to you."

There simply is a "differentness" about people who understand something of the mystery of Christ. It is not a bad "differentness," such as being so heavenly minded as to be of no earthly good; but it does involve a different life-style, a different set of values and marching to a different drummer from those who—Christian or not—are really living at a survival level.

God does not call us to survive. He calls us to eternal life.

QUESTIONS

1. Describe a Christian you know who always looks like he or she has a secret.

2. What is your favorite mystery about Christ that you carry in your heart?

3. Wherein is the element of mystery missing in your life, and what will you do about it?

4. How can we most effectively share the mystery of Christ with others?

17

The Faithfulness of Christ

Father Andrew, that great English monk, knew about faith. His statement about the "opportunity of faith" has strengthened me many times when I have been discouraged. He said:

> We have to remember that we shall never have this life again. We shall pass to other conditions, but in this life we have a unique opportunity of serving God and our neighbor in a particular way, and that will never come to us again. It is well for us to remember that we have our opportunity here and now to witness to God in this world and to do our part as well as we can while there is time. This life is the opportunity of faith. When we can see God, we shall be able to give him our worship and our love, but we shall no longer be able to give him our faith. That belongs to our period here.

If we are honest, we have to realize that not many people seem to seize the opportunity of faith that God gives us. We need only look around us, even among our Christian friends, perhaps in our own lives, to see that faith is often shallow and rootless.

When we look to Christ as our example, however, we see the ultimate in faithfulness. His life—and death—show us unswerving faithfulness. In Revelation he is called "the faithful witness"

(1:5), "Faithful and True" (19:11). In the Epistle to the Hebrews he is faithful as our high priest before God (2:17); and the Second Letter to the Thessalonians tells us that the Lord is to be trusted (3:3).

If we have a conception of what Christ did for us on the cross, we can have no doubt of his faithfulness. How then, can we be faithful? How can we reflect that kind of hope in a world that seems either to doubt or not to care?

There are at least three characteristics demonstrated in Christ's life that tell us about faithfulness. These characteristics also have been reflected in the lives of Christ's followers down through the centuries. They are: (1) knowing God, (2) growing in relationship with him, and (3) building the faith of others.

Faithfulness must be founded on a relationship. We can't be faithful to something that is meaningless to us. Christ who had the most faithful relationship with God the Father, also had the closest relationship with God the Father.

Our churches are filled with people who have never come into a meaningful relationship with God; many don't even know that the possibility of relationship exists. They have what might be called a "membership faith." They belong to the church as one might belong to a club or civic organization. Because no real encounter with God has been involved in their faith process, it is easy for them simply to drift away; or, if they remain attached to the church, their witness is a weak and confused one.

People who have knowledge of God, on the other hand, find it much easier to be faithful. They know the one in whom they have faith, and they know what he does for them and through them in their day-to-day lives.

A first step to faithfulness, then, is to know God. If we have never encountered him in a life-changing way, we should pray fervently that he will reveal himself to us. He will, if we truly want him to.

A next step is to be growing in the relationship of faith. For something to be alive, vital, active, it must be growing. We are not meant simply to learn certain basic information about the

Christian faith and then expect that to sustain us through the remainder of our lives.

Through regular worship, prayer, Bible study, Christian service, and in many other ways, we should be growing in our relationship with God. Our life-styles should profoundly reflect his influence upon us. Our priorities should be set in accordance with what we perceive to be his will for our lives. That is faithfulness in action.

Finally, faith increases in us as we seek to build faith in others. "Let us be firm and unswerving in the confession of our hope." (Hebrews 10:23). It is as we share with our Christian brothers and sisters what our Lord means to us that we build faith in them; and, as a wonderful side benefit, we realize that such "confessions of hope" increase our own faith.

Likewise, we can be reverse witnesses to our Christian friends. If we do not recognize the goodness of God's providence, but live according to the world's standards, we will be a negative witness. Nothing is as faith-destroying as a Christian whose words and actions belie the Lord who is supposed to be at the center of his or her life.

In the simple contacts of life, we walk a narrow line between opportunities of faithful witness and the danger of negative witness. If we want to seize the opportunities of faith to let people know why our lives are different, we must rely on Christ within us to guide our words and actions. His grace may abound in us to the blessing of those we meet, if we will only let him.

Some years ago, as I prayed about the question of Christian witness in my own life, the following "poem" came to me:

HE WILL NOT KNOW

I could give him reasons why I am
   a Christian,
But he could give me arguments

against those reasons.
I could tell him of spiritual
    experiences I have had,
But he could say they were my
    emotions.
I could tell him of physical
    healings I have had,
But he could say they were
    psychosomatic.
I could tell him of miracles
    I have seen,
But he could say they were
    my imagination.
I could tell him how, over and over again,
    things have worked out just right while
    I was following the Lord's leading,
But he could say they were
    coincidences.
I could tell him how relationships have
    been brought to wholeness,
But he could say that a psychological
    counselor could have accomplished
    the same thing.
I could tell him how lives
    have been changed,
But he could say they were simply
    attitude adjustments.
I could show him love,
But he could reject it.
If God has not gone before me,
To prepare his heart,
Nothing I could say
Would be of much value.
But if God has prepared his heart
and opened his eyes and ears
And I do not tell him why I am a Christian,

He will not know.
If I do not tell him of my experiences, my healings
and the miracles I have seen,
He will not know.
If I do not share with him the
ways in which Christ works in
my life and has worked in
the lives of others,
He will not know.
If I do not show him love,
HE WILL NOT KNOW.

QUESTIONS

1. When were you first conscious of God's presence in your life?

2. In what ways do you need to be growing in your relationship with God?

3. An example of a recent, positive witness of faith (by you or someone else) was:

4. An example of a recent, negative witness (by you or someone
   else) was:

18

The Friendship of Christ

"What a friend we have in Jesus," says the old hymn, and nothing could be truer. In the history of the world no example of friendship compares with Christ's. And, fortunately for us, it is an ongoing friendship in which each of us can share.

The nature of Christ's friendship is perhaps best stated in John 15:11-17:

> I have spoken thus to you, so that my joy may be in you, and your joy complete. This is my commandment: love one another, as I have loved you. There is no greater love than this, that a man should lay down his life for his friends. You are my friends, if you do what I command you. I call you servants no longer; a servant does not know what his master is about. I have called you friends, because I have disclosed to you everything that I heard from my Father. You did not choose me; I chose you. I appointed you to go on and bear fruit, fruit that shall last; so that the Father may give you all that you ask in my name. This is my commandment to you: love one another.

True, Jesus's friendship is conditional. In order to be his friend, we have to obey a command: "Love one another." But that command, in itself, is at the base of all friendship. It is not a selfish command; it is a prerequisite to freedom and life.

Jesus demonstrated the natural bonds of friendship in many ways, perhaps most dramatically in the story of Lazarus (John 11:1-44). He signed his own death warrant by going to Bethany (only two miles from Jerusalem where the Jewish leaders lay in wait to trap and kill him) and by so dramatic and provocative an act as bringing a friend back to life.

From what we know of Christ's friendship we may draw some conclusions about what a friend should be.

Christ made friends quickly. Since I became a Christian, I have been fascinated by how quickly I come into friendship with people whose lives reflect the life of Christ within them. If we free him to do so, Christ in us continues to make friends with Christ in others. I feel closer to Christians I have known for only a few days than I do to non-Christians I have known for years.

There is, of course, a simple explanation for this: Christians have, as a base of contact, the ultimate foundation because Christ is at the cornerstone of their lives. They have the ultimate secret, the ultimate friendship.

Christ shared with his friends the deeper things of life. He literally tried to pour his life into the lives of his disciples, that they might have as much of the fullness he had received from God the Father as they were capable of absorbing. "I have disclosed to you everything that I heard from my Father." (John 15:15).

Likewise, our friendship should be based on deep levels of trust in which we are free to share our joys and our sorrows. It has been said that it is only with our friends that we share the depth of our sorrows. If we allow Christ's friendship to flow through us, it will be friendship at a trusting, sharing level.

Real friendship is a give-and-take proposition. It involves mutual support, mutual giving, a balanced dependence upon one another. It was difficult for Christ to show us this principle by example because he was unique. He gave and gave, and it was impossible for Peter and the others to give anything comparable in return. But in laying down the command to love one another, Jesus made it clear that friendship was to be mutual.

Friendships can become unbalanced unless there is mutual giving. If one person, to satisfy his neurotic needs, must either do all the giving or all the getting, true friendship will not exist. Real friendship is based upon an openness and vulnerability to one another in which mutual sharing and support can take place.

Finally, true friendship involves being willing to lay down our lives for our friend. That is what Jesus did, and that is what the Christ in us would have us be willing to do. And that laying down of our lives will seldom be a one-time, life-giving action as Christ's was. It is more likely to be a nitty-gritty, daily giving of ourselves (perhaps primarily in listening to our friends) all our life long.

A few years ago I was on the receiving end of a message of what Christian friendship is all about. I had the problem of deciding whether to continue in the ministry in which I was then engaged. I went on a three-day fast to listen to what the Lord was saying to me. Just as I was about to decide that I was to continue the ministry, I received the confirmation I needed. On the final day of my fast I received a letter from a friend—written three days earlier—saying that he was just beginning a three-day fast on behalf of my ministry and what it had meant to him. Without knowing what I was doing, he fasted the same three days for the same purpose in my behalf.

QUESTIONS

1. An example of your immediately establishing a friendship with another Christian is:

2. What sort of things might be shared with a Christian friend? What things might not be shared?

3. How can you tell whether a friendship is properly balanced with mutual sharing, and what can you do if it is not?

4. One example of a person "laying down his life" for you is:

19

The Example of Christ

There are a multitude of ways in which Christ, as our example, is teaching us to live. Through his example, as seen in the Bible, he lets us know what it means to release his characteristics through our own lives, to make him incarnate within us that our example may be his example. First, however, we want to look at the nature of Christ as our example.

Initially, it is important to recognize that Christ is much more than simply an example. It is a grievous error for people to see Christ only as a good example, a person who set down some commendable principles by which anyone should want to mold his life. C.S. Lewis met that heresy head on when he said:

I am trying here to prevent anyone saying the really foolish thing that people often say about him: "I'm ready to accept Jesus as a great moral teacher, but I don't accept his claim to be God." That is the one thing we must not say. A man who was merely a man and said the sort of things Jesus said would not be a great moral teacher. He would either be a lunatic—or else he would be the Devil of Hell. You must make your choice. Either this man was, and is, the Son of God; or else a madman or something worse. You can shut him up for a fool, you can spit at him and kill him as a demon; or you can fall at his feet and call him Lord

and God. But let us not come with any patronising nonsense
about his being a great human teacher. He has not left that open
to us. He did not intend to.

Next, we should look at the kind of example Christ is. He is
an example to us on at least two levels. Certainly, he showed us
how we are to act and live by things he said and did. But, at a
much deeper level, he showed us, by his example, the nature of
God. Dr. William Barclay said that the supreme message of the
New Testament is not that Jesus is like God, but that God is like
Jesus. We could understand the fullness of the nature of God if
we could only understand Jesus in his fullness.

Scripture shows elements of this deeper meaning of Jesus'
example. Hebrews 3:1-6, for instance, reveals Christ as our
"Apostle and High Priest." In his own person he combines these
two positions. "As God, he has been 'sent forth' to reveal God
to man; as Man, he has become High Priest to reconcile men to
God." (*New Bible Commentary: Revised,* p. 1197). In this instance,
Christ was our example once and for all time. We cannot emulate
him in that regard.

Next, we are to understand suffering in light of one who
suffered and died on our behalf (1 Peter 2:18-25). Here Christ's
example gives us comfort in our suffering; but what he did in dying
for all mankind was not something that we can repeat. Again, it
was a one-time example in the history of the world.

Further, Christ teaches us an element of the deeper meaning
of his example when he says, "If anyone wishes to be a follower
of mine, he must leave self behind; he must take up his cross and
come with me." (Matthew 16:24). "The way of the disciple must
be the way of the master." (*New Bible Commentary: Revised,*
p. 839). In this manner, Christ gives us not a specific example
of how to carry out a particular act, but an everlasting call to a
new way of life—something we will only begin to comprehend
in its fullness as we "follow."

Finally, in Matthew 11:28-30, Christ says:

> Come to me, all whose work is hard, whose load is heavy; and
> I will give you relief. Bend your necks to my yoke, and learn
> from me, for I am gentle and humble-hearted; and your souls
> will find relief. For my yoke is good to bear, my load is light.

The deeper meaning of this example is that, if we will yield our
wills to the will of God—as we understand the will of God through
the revelation of Christ—we release Christ to share the load with
us, and he is willing and able to carry the bulk of it!

Having had an opportunity to look at the broader aspects of
Christ's example, how do we, in practical terms, follow him? By
carrying out the particular things he showed us to do and by
keeping our eyes on him.

In John 13:4-16, Jesus gave us a very specific example. In an
acted-out parable of sorts, Jesus washed the disciples' feet. In doing
so, his actions said, "You are here as servants; serve!" And, just
to be sure everyone got the message, he said, "I have set you an
example: you are to do as I have done for you" (John 13:15).

As I write these words, a major international sports event is
going on. Each day young people from all over the world are
competing "to win the race." They have had a host of examples
to look to in their training and in their execution of the sport.
They have seen how the great ones have done it, and they have
followed their techniques. They have gotten specific skills training
from noted teachers of the particular sport. But in the lonely
minutes of the actual race, they must reach for an inner strength
and determination that no earthly example or training can give
them.

So much more is that so in the race of life. The Epistle to the
Hebrews (12:1-2) tells us how:

> And what of ourselves? With all these witnesses to faith around
> us like a cloud, we must throw off every encumbrance, every
> sin to which we cling, and run with resolution the race for which
> we are entered, our eyes fixed on Jesus, on whom faith depends
> from start to finish: Jesus who, for the sake of the joy that lay

ahead of him, endured the cross, making light of its disgrace, and has taken his seat at the right hand of the throne of God.

If we are to reflect Jesus in our lives, if we are to make him incarnate among men, we must keep our eyes on him. He is our example for all time.

QUESTIONS

1. In what ways is it impossible for people to duplicate the example of Christ?

2. What are some of the ways in which we can follow Christ's example?

3. How do we respond to a person who thinks Christ was simply an example of how people should live?

4. What characteristic of Christ in the series has most profoundly affected your desire to free the Christ within you that you may make him incarnate in the world today? Why?

Section IV

The Heart of the Gospel

Introduction

Every passage in the Bible should be important to us either because of the historical information it conveys or the practical teaching we are to receive from it as Christians. For the person who has studied the Bible over the years, each reading of any portion of Scripture yields its own fruit of knowledge—giving historical perspective to help understand better the basis of our faith or a principle or principles of life to guide our walk of faith.

When we come to see the study of the Bible from that viewpoint, we are on the threshold of availing ourselves of the very best that the Bible has to offer. We don't look casually at the Bible as simply a great literary book, but as something with power and authority that will affect our lives.

There is the old story of what it would be like to inherit a million dollars. If my father had left a will in which I was heir to receive $1 million, and the terms and conditions of that bequest had been spelled out in the will, you can be sure that I would have read that will very carefully. I would have wanted to understand each pertinent provision as thoroughly as possible.

My life would have been greatly affected by that million-dollar gift, but not nearly as much as it has been and will be affected by a much greater gift from my Heavenly Father, the gift of eternal life through Jesus Christ. Further, there is a document which spells

101

out the terms and conditions of that gift from my Heavenly Father, and it is called the Bible. Should I not want to understand every pertinent passage in the Bible because of the effect that it has upon my life now and in the life to come?

We should study the Bible carefully, both for its historical value and its specific guidance in how to live. Although passages having to do with historical matters are important to us, those studies which reveal guidelines for living seem to be the most fulfilling, if we are willing to be guided by what God would teach us through the Bible.

Let us consider a particular method of Bible study as we attempt to survey "the heart of the Gospel"—those passages of Scripture which, in combination, give us a picture of Jesus's life, death, and resurrection.

1. *Background.* As we look at the passage of Scripture, we should try to understand the background in which it occurs. What is going on? Who is doing what to whom? This helps us to get the passage into its proper context.

2. *Perspective.* We should take a common sense approach to what we read, so that we can get it into proper perspective. We should avoid absurd conclusions or trivialities that have nothing to do with the heart of the message.

3. *Affirmation.* There may be in the passage, something that affirms us in the kind of life we are leading, that supports us and tells us that we are on the right track in following the Lord. What makes us feel good about the passage?

4. *Uncomfortable Truth.* On the other hand, we should look for "the uncomfortable truth" in the passage. What is said that threatens our complacency, that accuses us of sin, that shows us that God is calling us another step forward that we would just as soon not take? It has been said that Jesus came to comfort the afflicted and to afflict the comfortable. What gets my attention about the passage?

5. *Principle Involved.* We should next try to find the principle or principles involved. We should look below the surface of what has been said to discover the thing of lasting effect that should serve to guide us in the days and years ahead. What are the universal principles in the passage?

6. *Application.* Each of us should then seek the specific thing the passage says to us. What change or changes in my attitudes, habits and/or life-style is indicated by this passage?

7. *Resolution.* Finally, what are we going to do about what we have found? James 1:22 says, "Be ye doers of the word and not hearers only." Bible study is of no real value unless it leads us to resolve that we will be guided by what it has taught us.

In order to help us fix this method of Bible study more effectively in our minds, we will now explore a passage of Scripture using this method. Please read Matthew 6:24-34 in the Bible of your choice, and use the method set forth above as the means of studying the passage. I will share with you what I found in exploring the passage according to this method. I used the New English Bible for my study.

Background. As we can probably tell from our Bible, the passage is from Jesus's; "Sermon on the Mount." The setting is that Jesus is teaching his followers.

Perspective. He is not telling his followers to live exactly like birds or flowers in the sense of going around naked or with ragged clothes on, or not eating or earning a living. He is talking about the problem of anxiety.

Affirmation. I felt affirmation from the passage concerning my own vocation. Some years ago I left a well-paying job and promising future to go into a much less secure situation because I felt that that was what God wanted me to do. He has provided for me and for my family in the years since then, demonstrating the truth of what Jesus says in the passage.

Uncomfortable Truth. Despite God's providence, I do often worry about tomorrow. If I had as much faith as I would like to have, I wouldn't worry about tomorrow. I would look forward to the opportunities of tomorrow rather than the problems it may bring.

Principle Involved. To me, the basic principle involved in this passage is that we have a choice of either living in God's kingdom—under God's rule and protection—or being anxious slaves to the world.

Application. The application to me is that I need to stop wasting my time worrying. I need to use my time more constructively: to see what God would have me do, and to be more responsive to those around me.

Response. I put my response in the form of a prayer: "Lord, help me to reorder my life so that I live as a child of the Kingdom and not as a slave to the world."

Ten chapters—each covering a major aspect of the Gospel—are set forth for your study. With each you have a passage of Scripture to read, commentary on the passage (using the scholarship of the Bible Reading Fellowship) and my own "personalizing" of the lesson through some observations.

Whether this study is undertaken by members of a Bible study group, or by an individual studying alone, each chapter should be approached using the method of study set forth above. Because there are ten chapters in this final section, ten sessions of study are possible using "The Heart of the Gospel."

20

The Coming of the Kingdom

Read Matthew 3:1-12

Commentary: The voice of prophecy had been silent for centuries and the Jews longed for the time when God would act to deliver them from the Gentiles who had conquered their land. The appearance of John, dressed like Elijah of old (2 Kings 1:8) who was expected before the final Day of the Lord (Malachi 4:5) was a sensation. He spoke of imminent judgment. But it would mean the sifting of Israel rather than the destruction of the Gentiles. None was safe—neither the Pharisee who had been careful to separate himself from sinners and observe the Law to the last detail, nor the Sadducee who had worked to maintain the temple worship. Their sins had made physical descent from Abraham worthless. The only hope of salvation lay through repentance. The Jews had to confess their sins and, thinking of themselves as Gentiles outside the covenant, had to re-apply for admission to the true Israel by accepting baptism like proselytes (converts).

Matthew underlines the difference between John's baptism and Christian baptism. John's baptism is purely preparatory. It is a sign of repentance. There is no mention of forgiveness as in Mark. Christian baptism is the outpouring of the Holy Spirit (promised in Joel 2:28) which makes possible a new relationship with

God. But for the unrepentant there will be only the fire of judgment and destruction.

Observations: This passage contains both historical information (who was John the Baptist, what he preached, and his announcement of the coming of Christ and the effect thereof) and principles for application.

1. The only hope of salvation is through repentance, being truly sorry for the life we have lived and asking God's forgiveness.

2. John talks, however, about the fruit of repentance. If we do not become new creatures, as evidenced by lives changed for the good, are we truly repentant?

3. There is something without which the fruit of repentance cannot be sustained. Repentance may bring us into the Kingdom of God, but we can live in the Kingdom only through the power of the Holy Spirit within us. John brought repentance, but only Jesus can bring the Holy Spirit.

Background:

Perspective:

Affirmation:

Uncomfortable Truth:

Principle Involved:

Application:

Resolution:

21

God with Us

Read Matthew 1:18-25

Commentary: The Virgin Birth is not presented as a biological explanation of how Jesus can be both fully God and fully human. In fact, if the details are pressed too literally he would appear to be neither one nor the other. The incarnation is a miracle that must remain ultimately a mystery. But Matthew uses this story to express his faith that the hopes of Israel have found fulfillment and God himself is present among humanity in Christ. This child will save his people from their sins by inaugurating a new covenant (Matthew 26:28), and this is the work of God himself. In Christ's ministry and supremely in his death we see not only the obedience of a man with total trust in his Father but the love God himself has for the world—a love that cannot be expressed by proxy but only in person. As Paul affirms: "Christ died for us while we were yet sinners, and that is God's own proof of his love towards us" (Romans 5:8). Physically, Christ appeared to be the same as any other man, but as we read his Gospel Matthew hopes that his own faith will be born in us—that as we read the story of Jesus we will recognize not just the greatest of all religious teachers or the most devout of holy martyrs, but rather the one in whom God himself is present and active amongst his people, and, seeing this, one might be filled with wonder.

Observations: The passage starts off with simple words proclaiming a profound truth, "This is the story of the birth of the Messiah." The following thoughts appear significant:

1. Jesus will save his people from their sins. He will do it by his own death: a sacrificial lamb for the sins of the whole world. The price will be paid for our admission to the Kingdom. God loves us and will leave no stone unturned to lead us—each one of us—into the Kingdom, if we will let him.

2. Joseph is called to a very demanding level of obedience. We are told of two good qualities in him: (1) "he was a man of principle" and (2) he had compassion and forgiveness for one he had every reason to believe had treated him badly. But to expect him to accept the fact that Mary had become pregnant by the Holy Spirit was asking a great deal. God did not try to convince Joseph of this truth in a subtle way; he sent an angel. If we will let him, God will communicate with us in a way appropriate to the significance of the message.

3. The Law came from Moses, grace and truth came through Christ. We only had part of the message before God became incarnate; now we have freedom and fulfillment in Christ.

Background:

Perspective:

Affirmation:

Uncomfortable Truth:

Principle Involved:

Application:

Resolution:

22

The Temptation

Read Matthew 4:1-11

Commentary: The exaltation of spirit that Jesus experienced at his baptism when he received consecration to his messianic office was followed, as such moments of exaltation frequently are, by a time of testing, an experience of having the wind taken out of one's sails. It bears witness to the reality of his human nature as he grapples with the normal lot of temptation. As in his infancy, Jesus relives a historic moment in the history of his people. Israel spent forty years in the wilderness; Moses fasted forty days on Sinai when God revealed his will to him; Elijah traveled forty days toward the Mount of God. The figure of 40 has a symbolic significance, indicating a time of testing, a time of revelation. Jesus did not discuss the issue with the adversary. Was that not the original fault of Eve? He opposed the devil with the all-powerful weapon of the Word of God. He was so nourished by that Word that in the hour of temptation it sprang naturally to his lips. Bread, miracles, power—are not these what false messiahs in every age offer to the credulity of the crowds? Basically the temptations were to break the obedience to God's will in his mission that Jesus's Sonship must show. Like Moses on Mount Nebo, Jesus sees a promised land, the kingdoms of the world as God's Kingdom.

The Messiah heeded what Israel forgot, that any but God's way would mean simply a kingdom of this world.

Observations: Although the things that transpired in the passage happened to Jesus, there are principles that apply to us:

1. After revelations of the Spirit, we are often led into temptation. It is not God who leads us there, but Satan who would try to erase any spiritual gain we may have made.

2. Something that should never be forgotten about this passage—because it is so important for our future guidance—is that Jesus relied on Scripture to resist temptation and to refute Satan. Scripture was Jesus's source of spiritual authority, and it is also ours.

3. Yet Satan quoted Scripture to Jesus, so that Jesus had to show Satan truth through a fuller understanding of Scripture. This simply cautions us to have an ever-increasing understanding of the whole of Scripture and not just bits and pieces that suit us.

Background:

Perspective:

Affirmation:

Uncomfortable Truth:

Principle Involved:

Application:

Resolution:

23

Are You the One?

Read Matthew 11:2-11

Commentary: What a contrast between these two! The Baptist, fasting in the desert, warns of coming judgment when sinners will be consumed. Jesus, going to parties in the towns, announces a new life for all in trouble. Yet Jesus recognizes John as the Elijah who was expected to appear before the great Day of the Lord. Both John and Jesus were doing God's work in their different situations. Both believed in the goodness of God, announced his activity in the present age and called men to respond. People found excuses—rationalizations—to ignore them both. They put legal standing, religious observance, or nationalism before righteousness and preferred to carry on as Pharisees, priests, or zealots with their old ideas of God. They rejoiced that God had done great things in the past. They hoped that God would help them now. But the coming Kingdom proved altogether too upsetting and inconvenient. Even the Baptist, who had warned others to prepare, was hardly prepared himself for what actually happened. He had certainly been God's prophet, even the greatest. But God had overtaken him and moved ahead. The least in the Kingdom is greater than yesterday's man.

Observations: Here we have a passage that is both of historical significance (Jesus's affirmation that John the Baptist is the prophesied herald of the coming of the Messiah) and contains principles of life.

1. Isaiah 61 speaks of the effect of the Messiah's presence among the people (the coming of the Kingdom): captives set free, the binding up of the brokenhearted, liberty to the afflicted, comfort to those who mourn. Jesus, through his message to John, is saying that these things are happening. The Kingdom has come. As we see God's healing power manifested in our midst, we know that we are living in the Kingdom of God.

2. John the Baptist, as great as he was, is not as great as the least person in the Kingdom. I like to think of "great" here as meaning "well off." A person who realizes that he can live within the Kingdom of God and does so (though very imperfectly) is better off than John who (despite his major role in serving as the forerunner of Jesus) has doubts about the coming of the Kingdom.

Background:

Perspective:

Affirmation:

Uncomfortable Truth:

Principle Involved:

Application:

Resolution:

24

The Beatitudes

Read Matthew 5:1-12

Commentary: The Sermon on the Mount is the first of Matthew's great collections of Christ's teaching. Before and after it Matthew gives accounts of Christ's work of healing because it is only with the power of Christ to make us whole that we can face the challenge of life in the Kingdom—life under God's rule. The Sermon begins with blessing—not congratulations for the successful but encouragement for the weak. The man who has been beaten to his knees is blessed because he is in the right position to receive God's help; and God will help. Those who mourn a world apparently bereft of God and who ache for an end to oppression can rejoice because the power of God's justice is to be seen in Christ's ministry and resurrection. The gentle man who respects the weak can share the ministry of Christ who "will not bruise a broken reed" (Matthew 12:20) and, claiming nothing for himself, will enjoy the world that belongs to God (2 Corinthians 6:10). The merciful may still be cruelly treated (as Christ was himself) but they will share the forgiving fellowship of God. The pure in heart are those with a single purpose like the disciples who left all to follow Christ and who, in him, learned to see the Father. It is not those who merely desire peace but those who are prepared like Christ to make a sacrifice for peace who can share the work and the nature of God himself.

Observations: 1. Through the Sermon on the Mount, and in so many other ways, Christ calls us to see life from God's point of view. According to the things the world teaches us, God's ways often seem backwards—the opposite of what is easy and practical; but that is because we are looking at things through the short-sightedness of the world's narrow perspective. Christ would show us the fuller, richer way.

2. In the concluding sentences, Christ lays the matter on the line. He doesn't promise us a rose garden—only the thorns of persecution—but he gives us good reason to endure. Our reward will be eternal.

Background:

Perspective:

Affirmation:

Uncomfortable Truth:

Principle Involved:

Application:

Resolution:

25

The Transfiguration

Read Matthew 17:1-9

Commentary: Here is an incident illustrating Matthew's theme that Jesus is the new and greater Moses. When Moses went into the holy mountain he took with him Aaron, Nadab, and Abihu (Exodus 24). The face of Moses shone with a reflected glory, but Jesus's with the glory that would be his own. Moses and Elijah are the two witnesses to whom reference is also made in Revelation 11:3. Taken to heaven alive, they knew Jesus. They were expected to return to earth before the coming of the Messiah. The voice of God from the bright cloud, a sign of the divine presence as on Sinai, declares Jesus as the Son, the fulfillment of Old Testament expectation: with whom I am well pleased as in 3:17 means "in whom my plan for the world is centered." He is to be heard, for he will be the judge at the Last Day. Peter speaks rash words; he would have established the heavenly glory on earth (v. 4). Coming down from the mountain, Jesus enjoins silence on his disciples. What has been given to them is to fortify their faith in him, but not to be spread around as an amazing story.

Observations: 1. Here we see the "otherness" of Jesus. It must have been easy for the disciples to fall into the habit of thinking of Jesus as a human friend who had extraordinary powers. The Transfiguration reminded these friends that he was vastly more than that.

2. Peter's reaction to what happened was typical. Faced with something we can't handle, we so often want to "do something."

3. Spiritual experiences are given to us to increase our faith.

Background:

Perspective:

Affirmation:

Uncomfortable Truth:

Principle Involved:

Application:

Resolution:

26

Approaching the Crucifixion

Read John 17:1-26

Commentary: The "prayer of consecration" (John 17) sums up the farewell discourses of Jesus, and is John's equivalent of the prayer of Jesus in the Garden of Gethsemane just before his arrest (see Mark 14:32-42; and notice John 18:1f.). The prayer itself may well have been composed from a brief but authentic threefold petition which Christ offered to the Father as he approached death. For this prayer falls into three distinct sections, concerning Jesus himself (vv. 1-5), the disciples (vv. 6-19) and the church (vv. 20-26). At the heart of each prayer is the simple address, "Father" (vv. 1, 11, 24).

In the first section of this great prayer, Jesus consecrates himself (see also v. 19) in obedience to God. The moment of exaltation has arrived (v. 1); there is glory in the cross of Christ (see John 12:32). This means first that Jesus had completed the work of our salvation (v. 4; see 5:17; 19:28, 30). The life and ministry and death of Jesus together fulfilled God's purposes for us (see Acts 2:23), and made it possible for all men to receive his eternal life (v. 2). "Eternal" denotes a quality, not a quantity, and signifies our knowledge of God through Jesus (v. 3). A personal relationship with the Lord is implied here, not merely head-knowledge about him.

Secondly, there is glory in the cross because to finish God's work Jesus triumphed over sin and death; God raised and exalted him as Lord. For Jesus the cross meant going to the Father (John 16:28); for us it means life. Verses 6-29 describe the richness of Christian discipleship. (1) The disciple has been shown the name (or nature) of God by Jesus (vv. 6f). Christians are those who have come to know and obey the Father through Jesus the Son. (2) Jesus prays for his disciples. This implies a specially intimate relationship between God and the believer, meditated by the Son (vv. 9f.). (3) As Jesus brings glory to God and is glorified by him (v. 5), so the Christian can glorify Christ by living for him. (4) Those who belong to the exalted Christ belong to each other (v. 11). True unity begins with an attitude of acceptance and trust, not with ecclesiastical organization. (5) Disciples can draw on the resources of God in Christ for Christian living (see 1 Peter 1:3-5). (6) Christians are called to live in the world. They do not owe their spiritual rebirth or ultimate allegiance to it; in that sense they are called out of the world. They are "set apart" for God (v. 17). But Christians are still in the world; they are called to live responsibly in society, and (like Jesus) they are sent into it to pass on the Gospel to those in need. (7) The disciple knows Christ's gift of joy in the Spirit (see Galatians 5:22).

Observations: 1. Jesus's definition of eternal life is of utmost importance: to know God through Christ. Our acceptance of Christ and our relationship with God—his being a personal part of our lives—is eternal.

2. Jesus completed the work the Father gave him to do. We, also, are to complete the work God gives us to do.

3. Jesus made the Father known to those whom the Father gave him. We, too, are "given" children, spouses, and friends to whom God would be made known through us.

4. Jesus pinpoints his prayer toward those who have been given to him rather than for the whole world. This says something about concentrating our prayers on those matters which God places on our hearts rather than being vague and general in our prayers.

Background:

Perspective:

Affirmation:

Uncomfortable Truth:

Principle Involved:

Application:

Resolution:

27

He Is Risen!

Read John 20:1-10

Commentary: The Christian faith is an Easter faith. The basis of Easter is the indisputable fact, according to all four evangelists, that the body of Jesus, crucified and buried, disappeared from the tomb. John's account of the resurrection is very sober. Three witnesses to it are called, two of whom (Peter and John) discover the empty tomb for themselves (vv. 3-8). Notice the circumstantial details of v. 7: the body had gone, leaving the linen clothes undisturbed. We are dealing here not with delusions but reality; the resurrection is not a feeling but a fact.

But Easter is more than this. Christianity in the end is not the acknowledgment of an empty sepulchre. By itself this says very little. Built in the discovery of the empty tomb is a confession of faith in the risen Christ; the "sight" of the disciples was followed by belief (v. 8). Soon these apostles were preaching Christ, and at the heart of their message was the announcement that God had triumphantly raised Jesus from the dead (see Acts 2:22-36). Sin and death were conquered in the cross and resurrection of Jesus. Because he lives, we can live through him.

Easter is also a fellowship. To follow Jesus is to be in company with others who have risen to newness of life in him (v. 10). It is also to be in fellowship with Christ himself; and to share his daily presence and resurrection power for our lives and work.

Observations: 1. It was Mary Magdalene who came first. A chief sinner whom Christ had saved was early at the tomb. Jesus had said that the one who is forgiven much will be the more grateful (Luke 7:47), and this certainly applied to Mary. The fact is that we have all sinned much; and how grateful we are depends on the extent to which we have been able to perceive our sins and God's forgiveness.

2. Mary would not have been able to remove the stone from the tomb, yet she goes to anoint the body and the stone has been rolled away. So often we can find that true in our own lives. As we obediently go to do the work God has called us to do we find the "stone" that would block our pathway rolled away by God in ingenious if not miraculous ways.

3. The passage next faces us with the utter loss experienced by Mary. It is not enough that her Lord has been crucified; now there is not even a body to prepare for proper burial. We often have to reach that level of despair before hope can dawn in our lives.

4. At last the disciples get the message that Jesus had been preaching to them for quite some time: the Messiah was to rise from the dead. We shouldn't be too smug about the blindness of the disciples in understanding Christ's message. We are in a post-resurrection time, and, until that moment, they had not been. We know things that they did not; we must realize that today we know many things that others do not, and we must be patient with them.

Background:

Perspective:

Affirmation:

Uncomfortable Truth:

Principle Involved:

Application:

Resolution:

28

Peace Be with You

Read John 20:19-31

Commentary: The risen Christ sends out his disciples on a new mission, corresponding to his own (v. 21). They are to tell others about the life that Jesus gives, and for this purpose they receive a special gift of the Spirit (v. 22; this is John's anticipation of Pentecost, Acts 2:1-4). The Spirit who rested in Jesus himself during his ministry (see John 1:32f.) now baptizes the apostles. The proclamation of the Gospel by any disciple is a responsible business, involving as it does the offer of life in Christ or death without him (v. 23).

Who does not sympathize with the desire of Thomas for proof that Jesus is alive (vv. 24-29)? But even with the evidence at hand, he still needed to believe (vv. 27f.) What was true for the first disciples can be true for us today.

Observations: 1. Jesus meets his disciples at their point of need. They were fearful ("behind locked doors") and he brought them peace.

2. The imparting of the Holy Spirit was not only a giving of guidance, strength and power, it vested authority—the authority of the Kingdom of God in those who received it.

3. We still want to "see" in order to believe; that is not bad in itself. God will graciously show us if we truly want to see. But blessed are those whose faith is so strong that they require little "show me."

4. John's Gospel is written as a book of faith, that others may believe. We should write the "book" of our lives that others will have faith in Jesus as we do.

Background:

Perspective:

Affirmation:

Uncomfortable Truth:

Principle Involved:

Application:

Resolution:

29

The Great Commission

Read Matthew 28:16-20

Commentary: As the church looked back to the resurrection it was reminded that there was work to be done in the present. Matthew stresses that the risen Christ appears to his disciples to give them their instructions. It is remarkable that these men who failed Christ so miserably should be greeted as his brothers and entrusted with a world mission that makes Christ's previous ministry in Palestine seem almost insignificant. They must go to people of all nations, races, and faiths. They must baptize, drawing human beings into a new community of the Spirit as adopted children of the Father and brothers and sisters of Christ. They must teach, and it is for this teaching that Matthew's Gospel was written with its great collections of Christ's sayings—in particular the Sermon on the Mount. Here people will learn how life is to be lived and the presence and power of Christ will make it a reality.

Observations: Although brief, this passage is Christ's Great Commission, one of the most important instructions our Lord gave us.

    1. Full authority has been granted to Christ by the Father, and that is the authority which Christ now conveys to his followers.

2. "Therefore, go." That authority is to be used to reach all people.

3. People are to be baptized (brought into the household of faith) and taught. Those are dual, essential responsibilities; and the church is not as strong as it should be because we have so often failed in one or the other.

4. As we go about his work, as we live in accordance with his instructions, Christ is with us—whenever, wherever, forever.

Background:

Perspective:

Affirmation:

Uncomfortable Truth:

Principle Involved:

Application:

Resolution: